Tips & Tricks
For Toy Train Operators

Peter H. Riddle

GREENBERG BOOKS
A Division of Kalmbach Publishing Co.

Publisher's Cataloging-in-Publication Data

Riddle, Peter

    Tips and tricks for toy train operators / Peter H. Riddle
    p. cm.
    Includes index.
    ISBN 0-89778-395-6

    1. Railroads—Models. I. Title.
TF197.T69 1994   625.1'9
                  QBI94-2365

Contents

Introduction

Recently I tried to estimate how many layouts I have built over nearly half a century of fascination with miniature trains. The total must be measured in dozens, even if you don't count the temporary Lionel empires that wound beneath the furniture in my bedroom when I was but five years old.

My first serious effort came before I was in my teens: a round-the-wall tinplate pike on benches provided by my dad in the basement of our home. Upon entering high school I, like so many other teenagers in the 1950s, abandoned my Lionels in favor of the scale realism of HO. Throughout college I managed to find time to assemble a few kits and buildings in my dormitory room, even though I had no place to run them.

Graduation and marriage to my wife, Gay, followed our college years. Our first home was small, but we did have a small point-to-point HO pike.

There followed a succession of career changes for us both, necessitating a number of moves, followed by post-graduate study, and finally a relocation to the Province of Nova Scotia, where I most recently served as Director of the School of Music at Acadia University. Every home, rented or owned, had a train room of some description, and with every move the layout was completely dismantled, only to be reborn in a new format at the next address.

Gay and I sold our entire HO scale collection in 1984, having rediscovered the joys of toy trains. Since that time we've created at least a dozen tinplate layouts; after all, the joy is in the building, not in the having. Today our basement contains two permanent layouts, one in O gauge and one in Standard. The living room holds my wife's fully detailed Lionel Junior empire, a single loop in a fold-out cabinet just 3 feet square.

In my office at the university, a hollow-core door supports a prewar Lionel railroad town over the computer station, and in my wife's office in the Student Center (she's Director of Conference Services), her N scale Chesapeake & Ohio occupies the top of a filing cabinet. We also have a portable pike.

Thanks to all this layout-building, we've picked up a few tricks we'd like to share. I've forgotten the source of most of them, but would like to thank those many anonymous modelers who have shared their knowledge over the years, personally and through the pages of such magazines as *Toy Trains, Model Railroader, Railroad Model Craftsman, O Scale Railroading,* and especially *Classic Toy Trains.*

There are, however, certain ingenious tricks that came more recently from friends in the hobby, and I have credited these people wherever possible. Some of the ideas are truly original and inventive, and it pleases me to pass them on to you. Others are so obvious that I found myself saying, "Why didn't I think of that?" And finally, some are my own creation, developed from the decades of enjoyment that miniature trains have brought me.

Many of these ideas require no special equipment or supplies. The few needed items can be found in stores at the average shopping mall, and I've tried to steer the reader to sources wherever possible.

Specific toy train items are available from the many suppliers who advertise in the model railroad press or through such clubs as the Train Collectors Association (TCA), the Toy Train Operating Society (TTOS), and the more specialized clubs, such as the Lionel Collectors Club of America (LCCA), devoted to specific brand names. I highly recommend membership in these associations for many reasons, among them knowledge and information, buying and trading, and especially the good fellowship of new friends.

Many people have assisted me in bringing this work to you. First and foremost is my talented in-house editor and proofreader, my wife, Gay Riddle. At the Greenberg Books Division of Kalmbach Publishing Co., the following people contributed many types of technical expertise necessary to bring this book to its final form: Dick Christianson, editor; Allan Miller, managing editor; Mary Algozin, copy editor; Kristi Ludwig, art director; and Rick Johnson, designer.

Dedication

This book is gratefully dedicated to my wife, Gay: my foremost proofreader and editor, my partner in toy train collecting and operating, and my very best friend for more than 30 years.

Chapter One

TRACK TRICKS

*T*oy trains look great on a shelf, and I have no quarrel with the many collectors who are content with static displays. But Lionel, Ives, Gilbert, and their lesser-known brethren designed their products to be operated, and I have a special love for trains that spend their lives fulfilling this function. To do this, of course, they need track.

1 Painted Track Screws

Shiny screw heads detract greatly from the appearance of tinplate track on a layout, but they almost vanish when painted to match the ties. To paint them quickly, make a T-shaped support out of two pieces of wood, drive several dozen screws partway into the wood, and spray their heads with enamel (black for O or Standard gauge, medium brown for O-27, and dark brown for GarGraves). Painted heads all but disappear into the "woodwork."

2 Starter Holes in Wooden Ties

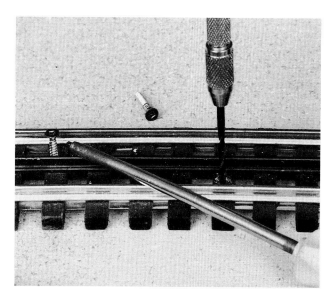

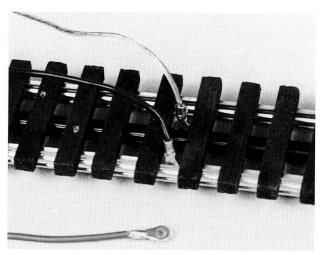

The GarGraves Trackage Corp. (8967 Ridge Road, North Rose, NY 14516-9793) manufactures an excellent line of flexible track mounted on stained wooden ties. The easiest way to install their track is by running small screws through the ties into the train table. But be careful! GarGraves track ties split easily and look unrealistic when they do. Before installation, drill a slightly undersized hole in each tie that will be screwed down. This prevents splitting when the screw is driven. It takes a little extra time, but the end results make the time well spent.

3 Hidden Track Wiring

Use of Lionel's track lockons makes wiring a layout easy, but these devices detract from the realistic look of a layout. My approach to making track connections does away with lockons, is equally simple, and hides the connections from view.

The rail of most toy train track, including GarGraves, is hollow, with a slot in the bottom: the cross-section resembles the Greek letter Omega. Before installing the track on the layout, force a short length of stiff solid-core

wire into the slots on the underside (you may want to use a small screwdriver to spread the rail a little), one in the middle rail and one in one of the outside rails.

For a positive connection, you may want to solder the wire in place in the slots, although this makes removal more difficult at a later date, should you decide to change the layout. A connection that is almost as secure can be made by crimping a spade lug on the end of the wire and forcing the lug into the slot in the rail, as shown. A lug is much less likely to work its way out than a single piece of wire, and its greater surface area will maintain better electrical contact, especially since the track is subject to vibration.

When you're ready to lay the track, drill holes in the tabletop at the proper places for these wires to pass through. When you have secured the track on the layout, these wires are very nearly invisible.

4 Making Insulated Track Sections

Lionel's pressure-type, under-the-tie contactors, designed for operating accessories such as crossing gates and highway flashers, are generally unreliable. A much more efficient approach is to use sections of insulated track placed at some distance from the accessories. Lionel has offered insulated sections over the years, but they're easy to make on your own.

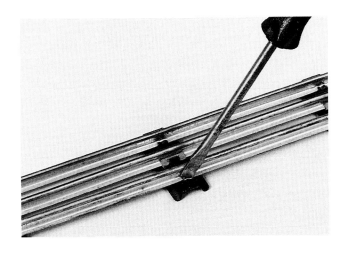

First, use a screwdriver to pry up the crimped portion of the ties that holds *one* of the outer rails, as shown in the above photo, and remove that rail. Then use a flexible non-conducting material, such as a thin automotive gasket, thin cardboard, or even a piece of electrician's tape, to make three insulators. Wrap them around the flanges of the rail where they meet the ties. The insulators must be carefully placed as shown in the photo above left so that when the rail is reconnected, there is no metal-to-metal contact between the rail and the ties.

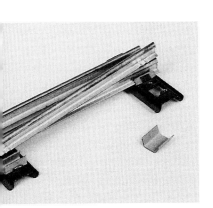

With the insulators in place, return the rail to its original location on the ties, and gently crimp the rail down with the screwdriver, just hard enough to hold the rail securely (photo below). Too much pressure can cause the fingers to penetrate the insulation. To be sure that the rail is truly insulated, attach a lockon to the track on the side with the *uninsulated* rail, connecting terminal 2 to the ground post of a transformer. Next, with the transformer turned on, touch the newly insulated rail with a wire running from any hot post on the transformer. If you get arcing, the insulation is faulty; if there is no spark, the outer rail is properly insulated.

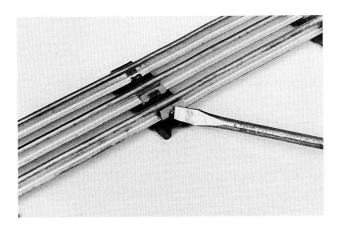

The final step is to insulate this rail from adjacent sections of track. Insert plastic or fiber pins in *both* ends of the insulated rail in place of the regular metal connecting pins. Lionel and other manufacturers market these insulating pins for use in both O and O-27 track.

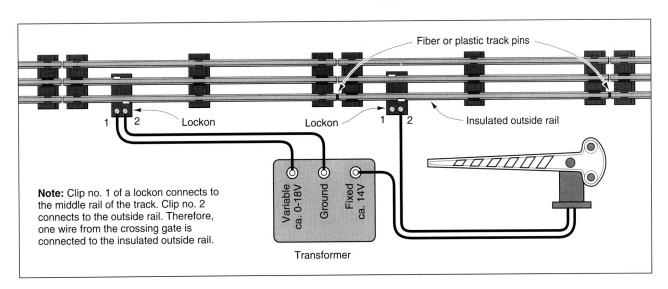

Note: Clip no. 1 of a lockon connects to the middle rail of the track. Clip no. 2 connects to the outside rail. Therefore, one wire from the crossing gate is connected to the insulated outside rail.

With the conversion complete, we can use this track section to operate automatic accessories. The diagram on page 7 shows how to wire a simple accessory such as a crossing gate. Note that the wire from the transformer delivers fixed voltage to the accessory. The other wire is a ground, but it isn't actually grounded until a locomotive or metal-wheeled car enters the insulated section of track. Then the ground connection is carried from the insulated rail through the wheels of the car to the other outside rail of the track, which is connected to the ground of the transformer.

Diagrams for operating other Lionel accessories can be found in Chapter Four, "Wiring Wizardry," of this book.

5 Accessory Control Using GarGraves Track

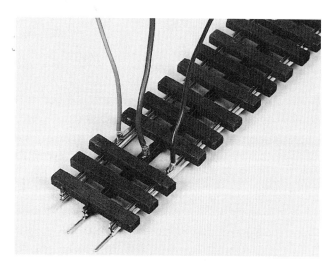

If you are using GarGraves track, note that all *three* rails are insulated from one another by the wooden ties. On conventional tinplate track, the two outer rails are electrically connected by the metal ties. This feature automatically gives you ready-made insulated track sections for operating accessories.

Install insulating track pins in the ends of one of the outside rails on every 3-foot length of GarGraves track. It's best to standardize in advance; on my layout, I insulate all rails that are toward the center of the table. Solder a short lead wire to each of the three rails, drill

holes in the table for these wires to pass through, and install the track. Use one color of wire for the middle rail (e.g., red), a different color for the insulated rail (I use green), and a third color (black) for the rail to the outside of the table.

Do the same for each successive length of track until you have finished a section of the layout. Don't forget to install insulating pins in the center rails wherever you plan to have independent blocks.

Now you have a loop of track completely installed and ready to be wired. Connect the *outermost* rail (black wires) to the ground post of the transformer and the *middle* rail (red wires) to the hot post. Leave the wires from all sections of the *innermost* rail (green) unconnected. The trains will now run, as they receive power from the middle rail and are grounded to the continuous outside rail that faces the perimeter of the table.

Next, complete the layout and install your automatic accessories (crossing gates, bells, gatemen, etc.) wherever they fit your plan. To make them operate, run a fixed-voltage hot wire (e.g., 14 volts) from the transformer to one terminal on the accessory. Connect the *other* terminal to the green wire from the nearest GarGraves track section.

The accessory should not operate by itself at this point, even when the power is turned on, because it is not grounded. The rail with the green wire is isolated from the rest of the track by the wooden ties and the insulating pins in its ends.

However, when a train arrives on that section of track, its metal wheels bridge the gap between the grounded outermost rail and the insulated rail. The ground is completed and the accessory operates. If you have connected a crossing gate at this point, it will stay down until the train has completely left the section of track to which it is connected.

The biggest advantage to this system is its flexibility. If you install an insulated rail in *every* section of GarGraves track, you can add an accessory at any point on the layout at any time without having to go through the mess of ripping up trackwork.

6 Secure Mounting of Lionel's Bumper

7 Standard Gauge Bumpers

Lionel's bumper, such as model no. 260 shown in the photo, has two screws mounted on the forward end. The idea is that when the bumper is in place on the track, these screws may be tightened against the rails. Unfortunately, they don't do a great job of holding the bumper firmly to the track.

Especially on lightweight O-27 track, even a slight jar from a locomotive or car can dislodge these bumpers. Keeping them in place is easy. Remove the screws entirely and place the bumper in position on the track. With the tip of an awl through each of the screw holes, scratch a mark on the side of the rail.

Remove the bumper and drill a hole through the rail at the marked point. Loosely reinstall the screws in the bumper, put it back on the track, drive the screws completely into the drilled holes in the rails, and the bumper will stay put through anything up to a 7 on the Richter Scale.

Although Lionel's no. 025 bumpers for O gauge track are fairly common and easily found at train meets, the large model 25 for Standard gauge is often quite scarce. The O gauge version can be made to fit on Standard gauge track, however. This model fits easily *between* the outer rails instead of over them, as when used with O gauge track.

Two machine screws are designed to be tightened against the outside of the outside rails of O gauge track. Instead, loosen them by turning counterclockwise, until the heads project at either side enough to press against the *inner* surfaces of the Standard gauge track. Then slide the bumper into place as shown in the photo.

If you want an extra-secure installation, drill a hole through the rail opposite the location of the screw hole in the bumper. Then insert a long screw through the rail and into the hole in the bumper. This is similar to the method described in the previous entry for O gauge track; the difference is that in this case the screw enters the rail before being threaded into the bumper.

8 Hidden Trackage

If your layout has hidden loops beneath the main table, you may want to mount them on open lattice-work hangers instead of on a solid table. This allows greater working room under the table, although you must be careful to avoid hitting your head on the hangers.

Screw lengths of 1 x 2 spruce to the stringers that support the table above. Place a crossbar at the required height of the track. If the hangers are close together, you may want to screw the track directly to the crossbars, but for longer runs, ¼"-thick boards should be used for extra support.

9 Toggle Controls for Lionel Switches

The control boxes for Lionel switches are bulky and take up a lot of room on a control panel. Miniature toggle switches take up a lot less space and are easy to install. You will need

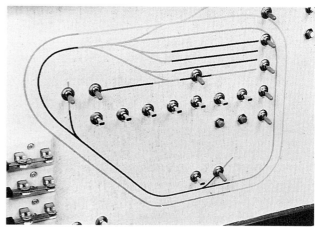

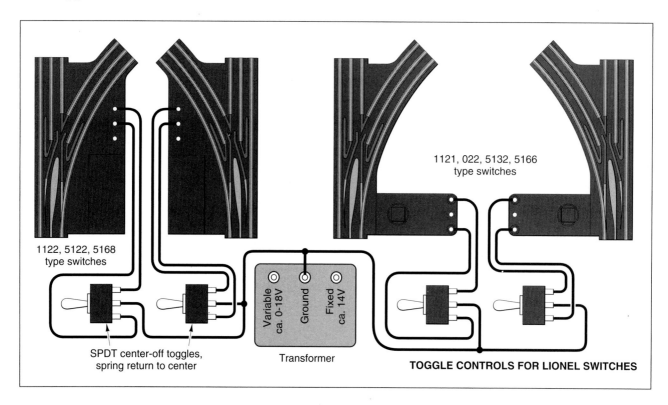

1122, 5122, 5168
type switches

1121, 022, 5132, 5166
type switches

SPDT center-off toggles,
spring return to center

Variable ca. 0-18V Ground Fixed ca. 14V

Transformer

TOGGLE CONTROLS FOR LIONEL SWITCHES

a single pole, double throw (SPDT) toggle with a center-off position and a spring return to center. This type of toggle is normally off. Pushing it in one direction completes the circuit to one wire; pushing it the other way directs current to a second wire. When your finger releases the toggle, it turns off automatically.

Connect the middle pole of the toggle to the ground wire from the transformer (the same as the wire that connects to the *outside* rails of the track). Connect the two outer poles of the toggle to the terminals on your Lionel switch, as shown in the diagram on page 10. When current is reaching the switch solenoid, either through the track or via a fixed-voltage plug, operating the toggle will operate the switch.

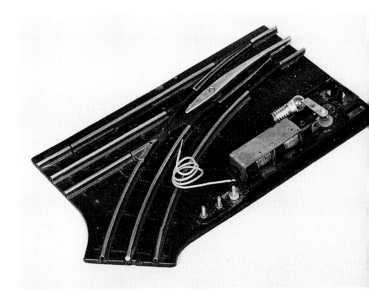

10 Fixed-Voltage Wiring for Switches

Lionel switches, especially the O gauge no. 022 models, need a fairly strong shot of current to operate positively. If they derive their power from the track, and if the trains are moving slowly at low voltage, there may not be enough current to ensure that the points snap securely to the proper position.

The 022 switch shown in the photo is provided with a fixed voltage plug. Connect this plug to a transformer's fixed voltage post that provides at least 14 volts. Regardless of the amount of voltage being fed to the track, this plug will always supply the turnout with enough current for a snappy response.

Lionel's O-27 switches, such as the no. 1122 in the photo (above right), are not provided with fixed-voltage plugs. It's fairly easy to modify them, however. Take off the solenoid housing and locate the wire that connects the solenoid with the middle rail. Solder it to a length of 18-gauge wire, and connect it to a fixed-voltage post of at least 14 volts. Now it will operate reliably under any conditions, just like its big brother, the 022.

11 Fixed-Voltage and Ground Wiring for Uncouple/Unload Ramps

Lionel's UCS, RCS, nos. 1019, and 6019 uncouple/unload ramps operate from track power, just like the switches described in tip no. 10. One of the four wires that leads to their control boxes is there simply to provide power from the middle rail; another grounds to the outside rails.

The major disadvantage to this system is the requirement that power be present in the track when the ramps are activated. For example, if one of Lionel's nos. 3472 or 3662 automatic milk cars is being unloaded at its platform, the locomotive must stand in neutral (with its E-unit buzzing) so that sufficient power reaches the accessory.

This is only a minor inconvenience with locomotives that have three-position E-units and can stand in neutral. With the two-position E-units that are found in some lower priced locomotives, it makes using such accessories all but impossible.

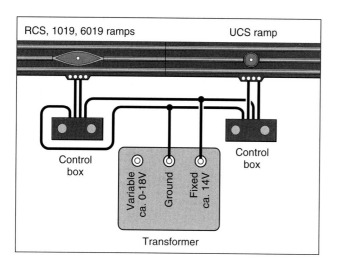

The solution is to provide the ramps with fixed voltage. The diagram shows which wires to connect: the one at the left on RCS, 1019, and 6019 ramps, and the one on the right on UCS ramps.

Similarly, a ground wire may be connected directly to the control box as shown. The main advantage to this is that it eliminates a wire between the ramp and the controller. If connected in this manner, all control boxes can be powered and grounded at the control panel, and only two wires need be routed to each uncouple/unload ramp.

12 Automatic 1121 Switches

Many Lionel switches are nonderailing, automatically switching to match the route of an oncoming locomotive. However, model no. 1121, made for a few years before and after World War II, does not have this feature. Nevertheless, I have many of them on my layout. Since it is built without conventional frogs or guardrails, the 1121 can accommodate my early American Flyer locomotives that have very large gears on the backs of the drivers and will not pass through the guardrails on Lionel nos. 1122 or 022 switches. Most Marx locomotives also have problems with frogs

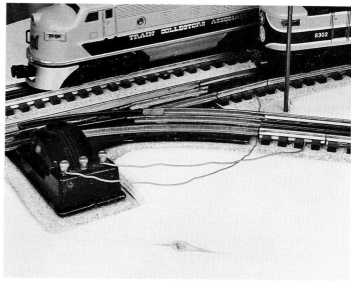

and guardrails, but they operate on 1121 switches without difficulty.

Fortunately, it's easy to add the nonderailing feature to an 1121 switch. Install a section of track with an insulated outside rail at each of the approach locations, curved and straight. Then run a wire from the insulated rail on the curved side to the outside terminal that throws the switch curved. Repeat the process for the straight side, as shown in the photo. As soon as a locomotive or car enters the insulated section, its metal wheels will complete the ground and cause the turnout to move in the correct direction. These wires may be used in addition to regular Lionel control box connections; they have no effect on manual operation.

The switch shown in the photo has been installed in a reverse loop at a hidden location under my layout. Since its only purpose is to send a train back in the opposite direction, it doesn't matter which way it is thrown when the train enters from the point side, and no control box is necessary. It operates only in response to a train approaching from the frog side, either on the curved or straight leg.

13 Modifying 1121 Turnouts for O Gauge Trains

Lionel model no. 1121 switches are especially useful for operators of prewar equipment, as they lack guardrails and will allow the passage of a wide variety of wheel sizes. American Flyer and Marx locomotives with large gears on the drivers will operate on them but will not work with 1122 or 022 types. Prewar flanges and wheelset gauges differ widely as well, and these switches will accommodate almost any variation.

Most of the large Lionel O gauge locomotives can handle the tight 27"-diameter curve of the model 1121, including even the big prewar nos. 260 and 263 steamers and postwar F3 diesels.

Even the *Flying Yankee* and *City of Denver* streamliners can manage the curve, but the housing over the switch solenoid mechanism is too high and too close to the track, and the locomotives' belly pans hit it when these trains take the curved route.

Fortunately there is an easy way to modify the switch housing. Using a fine-tooth saw (a hacksaw or razor saw is best), cut ½" off the upper part of the housing. There's still plenty of clearance for the solenoid mechanism. Dress the cut edges with a file, then use black electrician's tape to cover the opening. (The cut side may be left uncovered, but then the interior lamp will shine through the opening.) When this small amount of the housing has been removed, even the large prewar streamliners have enough clearance to negotiate the switch.

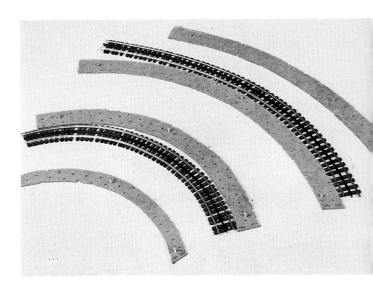

GarGraves flexible track is a well-made product that greatly improves the appearance of a train layout. The low profile, closely spaced wooden ties, and blackened center rail eliminate the toylike appearance of sectional track, and the T-shaped cross section of the rails improves performance. Flexible track also allows one to avoid the geometric appearance of layouts built with sectional track of fixed radii. The main drawback to its use is the difficulty of bending smooth curves without kinking the track.

Many ideas have been suggested in the past, from bending the rails around one's stomach to using a water heater as a template, but there is a more satisfactory method—a track-bending jig. Although it takes some time to set it up, the time saved in bending the track more than makes up for it.

On a large square of plywood, about 3 feet square, mount a series of templates cut to standard diameter measurements. Each template has two sides, and four or five of them will give you a wide choice of diameters. For example, the largest template on my jig, shown in the photo, measures O-72 on the outside (6-foot diameter curve) and O-64 on the inside (5'-4" diameter). The smallest is for O-27 curves, and there are also patterns for O-31 (standard O gauge track), O-42 (a common

Lionel and K-Line measurement), and several other dimensions.

These templates, cut from pegboard, are held to the plywood by three screws each, for easy removal. This allows them to be placed on the layout for a final alignment check during installation of the track. The track is bent by pressing its ties against the appropriate curve gently and with a slow and steady pressure. Since track has a tendency to straighten slightly after bending, you may want to bend it to the next smaller diameter first, and then ease it back to the desired dimension.

After bending, the inside and middle rails will be longer than the outside one and must be cut to match the end of the next adjoining section. A razor saw or fine-toothed hacksaw works well, or you can use rail nippers for this purpose. The cut ends will need some re-shaping with pliers and dressing with a file to make them smooth.

15 Laying Concentric Curves with Flexible Track

The track-bending templates described above can also be used to maintain a constant distance between two curved main lines. In the example shown in the photo, the outer curve is O-72 and the inner one O-64. This 8" difference provides a space of 4" between the center rails, adequate clearance for most O gauge toy trains.

Place the template between the inner and outer sections of track during installation. This maintains a constant curvature as the track is screwed down, as well as a constant distance between the two concentric curves. Move the template along the route as you continue laying track, guaranteeing a smooth and even curve.

16 Transition Curves with Flexible Track

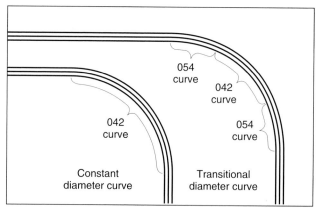

Sectional toy train track is built to a fixed diameter, and this diameter is constant throughout the length of each curved section. Prototype railroads, however, have gradual curves, which begin to bend slightly and do not reach the sharpest bend until the middle of the curve. This gradual easing into the curve is called the *transition*.

When you're bending flexible track, the ends that mate with adjacent straight sections should be bent to a larger radius than the center of the curve. For example, if you want an O-42 curve (42" in diameter), bend the beginning and end of the curve to approximately 54" or even 58".

When installing the track permanently, make further adjustments to create a gradual transition in diameter, rather than an abrupt change. This not only looks more realistic, it also provides smoother performance, as locomotives do not slam into a curve of abruptly changing radii.

17 Transition Curves with Sectional Track

Smooth transition curves can be approximated with sectional toy train track by combining different radii. In the example shown in the photo, two diameters of Standard gauge track are used: 42" and 72". One section of 72" starts the curve, a section of 42" forms the middle, and a final section of 72" completes the 90-degree corner.

Not only do the trains perform better on these gentler curves, they also look much better. Sudden changes of direction are typical of toy trains on sectional track, and these transition curves minimize the abruptness of entering a tight-radius circle. Standard gauge track in these two diameters is available from

Antique Trains, 1 Lantern Lane, Turnersville, NJ 08012. The same effect can be accomplished by combining O-31 (standard O gauge) and O-42, O-42 and O-54, O-54 and O-72, or O-27 and O-42. These sizes are available from such manufacturers as Lionel and K-Line.

18 Magnets Keep Light Cars on the Track

My wife Gay gets credit for this one. Having just finished repairing an 80-year-old Bing locomotive, I was testing it on the track and quickly discovered that the very light four-wheel tender would not stay on the track at any speed above a crawl. It was just too light and bounced off the rails at every irregularity of the track.

My first reaction was to remove the body from the frame and pack the interior with enough weight so the tender would stay on the track. However, I was reluctant to bend the metal tabs that hold the body on, as they are easily broken. As I studied the problem, looking for a sophisticated remedy, Gay gave me a simple, instant, and perfect solution. "Stick a magnet to the bottom of the frame between the wheels," she said.

Of course, her suggestion worked perfectly. As is so often the case, the answer was KISS: Keep It Simple, Stupid.

19 Hidden Track Detection Lights

One of our layouts is a variation on the displays that Lionel built in the early 1950s. My wife and I call it our "Magic Railroad," and it delights kids and adults alike.

At one end of the 4 x 8 table is a short tunnel (see photo on page 17). A long freight train thunders toward one end of the tunnel, while from the other direction our tiny Canadian Pacific snowplow trundles toward what seems like an unavoidable collision.

The freight plunges into the tunnel straight at the approaching snowplow. The snowplow enters the tunnel and emerges unscathed from the other end. Astonishingly, the freight train has disappeared!

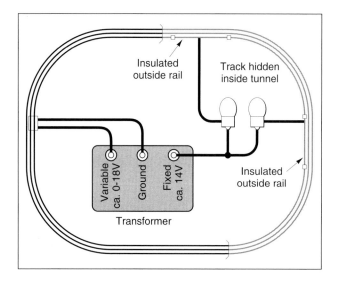

The secret, of course, is Lionel's powerful hill-climbing feature, Magne-Traction. The freight has been diverted through a switch, dropping to a hidden reverse loop beneath the layout. It's completely out of sight, but the operator knows exactly where it is at all times, thanks to a set of detection lights on the control panel.

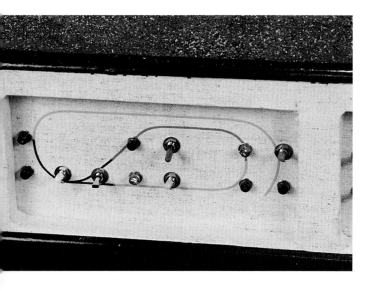

These lights are wired to sections of insulated outside rail spaced around the hidden loop of track and wired as shown in the diagram. As the train proceeds around the loop,

the lights come on in succession to show its exact location. Since the lights are powered by fixed voltage, they remain lit even if the train is stopped. This detection system lets the operator know a train is hidden away, warning against sending another train onto this invisible section of the layout.

20 The "Magic Railroad": A Hidden-Loop Track Plan

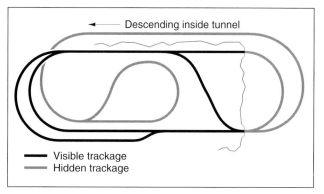

The track plan for the "Magic Railroad" described above is relatively simple. I built the hidden loop from sturdy Lionel O gauge track, descending into the interior of the table on a no. 110 trestle set. This reverse loop is powered by one throttle of a KW transformer, while the other throttle is used for the visible track on top of the table.

One train enters the tunnel in a counterclockwise direction, but instead of continuing through the tunnel, it is switched onto the lead to the hidden loop. Meanwhile, another train enters the tunnel heading clockwise. If the operator times it properly, the first train will be clear of the switch before the second one reaches it. I used a Lionel no. 022 nonderailing switch in this location, powered by fixed voltage. This prevents derailments inside the tunnel.

The photo on the next page shows the "Magic Railroad," with a seemingly imminent collision expected in the tunnel. Whether operated for a class of school children or a dormitory full of university students, it's proved to be a great crowd pleaser!

The "Magic Railroad," with its apparent imminent collision, depends on the magic of Magne-Traction.

21 | Lionel Magnets in GarGraves Track

Since the "Magic Railroad" was designed especially for younger audiences, it has a variety of Lionel accessories set up for the children to operate themselves. They can also uncouple the cars and dump loads of logs or coal from pushbuttons located around the perimeter of the table.

As the photo above suggests, I like the appearance of GarGraves track for display layouts. Unfortunately, Lionel's uncouple/unload ramps, such as the no. 6019, don't look the best when mixed in with GarGraves, especially on a small layout.

GarGraves sells sections of track with uncoupling magnets built in, and they work well. However, my Scottish ancestry rebelled at buying them when I had a couple of boxes

of old 6019 ramps stored away. The magnets proved to be easy to remove from these ramps and just as easy to install in lengths of regular GarGraves track.

The rails of a 6019 ramp are held in place by bent-over tabs on the underside. Pry them up until the rails can be lifted off, cut the two wires from the magnet, and remove the magnet. Lengthen the wires by soldering extra leads to them, and then wrap the core of the magnet with electrician's tape to ensure proper insulation.

Next, cut the middle rail of the track to leave space the same length as the diameter of the magnet. Cut the center out of the tie in this location. The tops of the rails should also be filed or cut to allow the plastic top piece of the magnet to be mounted flush, as shown in the diagram.

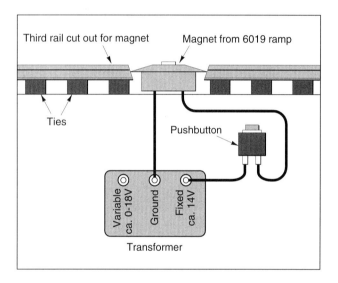

Measure carefully for these cuts in the rail and tie, so that the magnet will be held tightly in place by friction. With the track mounted on the layout, drill two holes in the tabletop for the wires, and put the magnet in place. You may wish to cement it in for security, although I have found that a magnet will stay in place if the fit is tight enough.

Connect one of the magnet wires to the ground post of the transformer and the other one to a fixed-voltage post through a normally off pushbutton. When the button is pushed, the magnet comes on and releases any Lionel coupler that passes over it. I used the KW transformer's 20-volt post, as it guarantees positive uncoupling on even the most stubborn uncoupler.

Other attractive features of the "Magic Railroad" are the two milk car platforms and the no. 3356 horse car and corral. These items also need Lionel control ramps—a regular 6019 section for the former and an OTC contactor for the latter.

Again reluctant to mix these Lionel units with GarGraves track, I made my own control rails from 1/4" aluminum ground cable from a radio supply store. This wire can be shaped easily into supplementary rails, as shown in the photo. Bend it at right angles at each end, drill 1/4" holes in the table between the ties, and insert the rails into the table so they lie just below the level of the track rails.

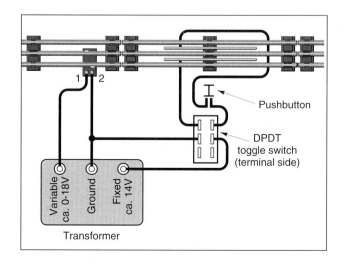

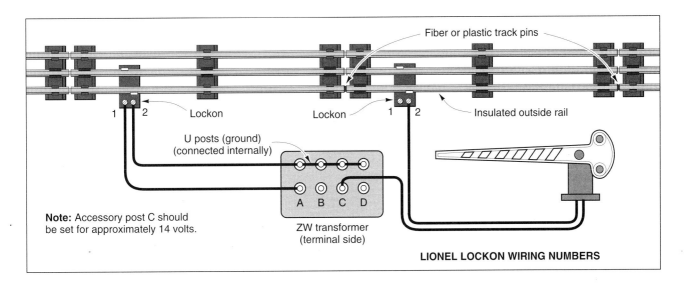

Note: Accessory post C should be set for approximately 14 volts.

ZW transformer (terminal side)

LIONEL LOCKON WIRING NUMBERS

One of these rails is grounded while the other receives power from a fixed-voltage post. The level of voltage depends upon the sensitivity of your operating cars. Twelve volts is usually about right, but not all transformers have this setting. If your horses gallop or if the milkman throws the cans clear off the platform, you may elect to use power from one of the throttles instead, adjusting it for optimum operation.

I use a double pole, double throw (DPDT) toggle, as shown in the diagram on page 18, so I can turn off these accessories from the main control panel. This prevents unsupervised operation by young observers. When the toggle is on, the pushbutton provided for the children will activate the milk or horse car.

Note that it is impossible to fasten wires to the aluminum ground cable using regular solder. Mechanical connections are satisfactory here. Simply strip an extra-long portion of the wire and wrap it around the ground cable several times. Hold it in place with electrician's tape.

23 Lionel Lockon Wiring Numbers

This is an elementary bit of information, but it should be noted by layout builders who use Lionel lockons. The wire clip labeled "1" on the typical Lionel lockon carries current to the *middle* rail. The number "2" clip is connected directly to one of the *outside* rails, and to the *other* outside rail as well through the metal ties of the track.

If you are using a section of track with an insulated *outside* rail to activate a relay or an accessory (see Chapters Two and Four for applications), a lockon attached to the *insulated* side may be used to attach the accessory through clip no. 2; this rail and the no. 2 clip on its lockon are isolated from the ground connection of the transformer.

The drawing below shows the correct way to wire a typical transformer (in this case a ZW) to the track through a lockon. Note that on a ZW or KW transformer, the "U" post is the ground and connects to lockon clip no. 2, while the throttle connection (A or D on a ZW, A or B on a KW) is wired to clip no. 1.

Also shown is a crossing gate wired to an insulated outside rail through a lockon; note that the lockon is on the same side as the insulated rail. (For more information, see "Wiring Accessories to Insulated Track Sections" in Chapter Four.)

Chapter Two

MOTOR MAGIC

*W*hen the first electric trains became available around the turn of the twentieth century, they must have seemed inexplicable and wonderful creations. Attached to mysterious wet or dry cells, and moving under their own power, they often constituted a family's first experience with modern technology. Today, nearly a century later, the vast majority of toy train motors operate under exactly the same principles as their primitive ancestors. And while they generally work pretty well, there are lots of little tricks that can help toy trains to perform their best.

24 Cleaning Commutator Faces

The easiest way to remove accumulated dirt from the segmented face of a motor commutator is with a pencil eraser. Its softness ensures that the plates will not be scratched, and the mild abrasive action of the eraser removes deposits completely. It is easiest to work on the commutator by removing the brushplate, but on most Lionel, Ives, or American Flyer motors, enough of the commutator is exposed to provide access even if the brushplate is left in place. Simply rotate the drive wheels gradually as you work, and the armature will rotate to let you clean the entire commutator. Be sure to blow away any tiny bits of rubber that flake off the eraser. If you do remove the brushplate, take time to use the eraser on the faces of the brushes as well. This simple procedure markedly improves the operation of toy train locomotive and accessory motors.

25 Adding Manual Reverse

Some inexpensive prewar locomotives, such as Lionel's nos. 150 and 248 models and the smallest Ives and American Flyer locomotives, were made to operate in the forward direction only and have no reverse lever. It's easy to add one, however, since these old motors will run in either direction if they are rewired properly.

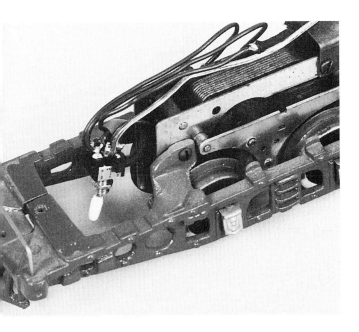

Prewar toy train motors are of the universal AC variety and can be made to run backwards by reversing the current to the brushes. (The same result can be obtained by reversing the current flow through the field winding, but the brush wires are more accessible.) All you need is a miniature DPDT (double pole, double throw) toggle switch and some short lengths of wire, as shown in the photo above.

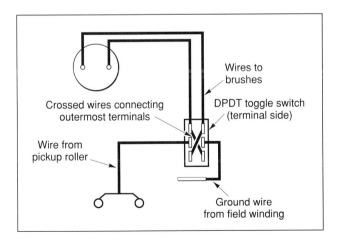

Wires to brushes

Crossed wires connecting outermost terminals

DPDT toggle switch (terminal side)

Wire from pickup roller

Ground wire from field winding

A DPDT switch has six terminals on the back. Disconnect the two wires that attach to the motor's brushplate, and reconnect them to the two *middle* terminals of the DPDT, as shown in the diagram. One of these wires comes from the roller pickup beneath the locomotive, while the other is a ground that passes through the field winding. Next, connect two wires between the brushes and two terminals at one end of the DPDT switch. Finally, connect two short wires in an "X" pattern between the outermost terminals of the switch, also shown in the diagram.

When the switch is thrown in one direction, power moves to the brushes exactly as if the original factory wiring had been retained. When thrown in the opposite direction, however, the "X" wiring reverses the current flow, and the motor runs backward. If you use a DPDT switch with a *center off* position, the locomotive can also be parked in neutral, even if there is power in the track. This is useful if you have two locomotives on the same track and you wish to leave one stationary.

Some locomotive frames may have a convenient hole for mounting the switch; if not, you may want to drill one in a suitable location. Should you not wish to alter the locomotive in any way, use very stiff *solid core* wires, at least 18 gauge or even 16 or 14 gauge, when making these modifications. This wire is stiff enough to maintain its shape without support and can be bent in such a way as to hold the DPDT switch suspended beneath the locomotive, out of sight but within easy reach of your fingers.

26 Replacing Insulation

The wiring in old toy trains is frequently found in a deteriorated condition, but the metal core of the wire is usually not the problem. Rather, the insulation tends to dry out and break off over time, leaving the wire exposed to short circuits through contact with the frame or other parts. The easiest and cheapest replacement for this insulation can be found in a pet store: aquarium air hose. This clear tubing comes in a variety of diameters and slips easily over bare wires or even over wires with damaged insulation still present. It cuts easily, and since it's transparent, one can be sure the wire inside is still intact. Just unsolder one end of the bad wire, slip a precut piece of tubing over it, and resolder.

27 Supplementary Pickups

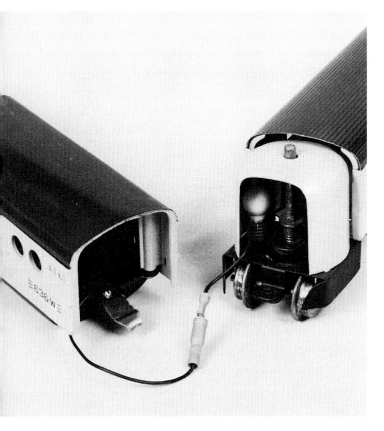

Except for some very old models, most toy train locomotives have two roller pickups to provide current to the motor. This enables them to pass over switches and crossings without losing electrical contact; when one of the rollers may be momentarily out of contact with the middle rail, the other supplies power. However, some very short locomotives may not have their rollers far enough apart to ensure constant contact. Some streamliners from the mid-1930s, such as the *Flying Yankee* and *City of Denver*, also have a short space between rollers and cannot maintain contact on some longer types of switches.

If a locomotive has a whistle tender, or if there is a lighted car (coach, searchlight car, etc.) with a roller pickup immediately behind the engine, it's easy to run a jumper wire from the car's roller pickup to the locomotive. This guarantees uninterrupted power to the motor under almost all conditions.

The photo shows such an installation on a Lionel *City of Denver* streamliner from the mid-1930s. The jumper wire is soldered to the motor's middle-rail contact shoe. The other end of the jumper is connected to the bracket of the middle-rail roller in the vestibule between the locomotive and the first coach. This roller supplies current to the light bulb in the vestibule; the jumper wire allows it to feed the motor also. On many of these roller brackets, there is already a screw provided for attaching a wire.

Note that there is a quick-disconnect plug mounted in the center of the jumper wire. This allows easy separation of the engine from the following car. On a streamliner, this plug is hidden inside the vestibule when the train is running. With a steamer, some ingenuity will be needed to conceal the wire beneath the tender. Use a small piece of electrician's tape to hold it against the bottom of the frame.

With this jumper installed, the motor now receives power from *three* pickup rollers instead of two. This ensures a constant supply of current, even when passing over complex patterns of switches and crossings.

28 Replacing Roller Pickup Assemblies

One of the most common parts needing repair on early toy trains is the locomotive's roller pickup plate. The rollers are suspended from thin pieces of sheet metal mounted on a fiber plate that fits between the sideframes of the motor. The roller mounts frequently break off. Fortunately, replacement pickup plates are available from parts suppliers. The replacement plates consist of the fiber bracket with two rollers already attached.

These brackets have four projecting fingers, two on each side, designed to fit into slots in the motor frame. However, the metal from which the motor is made is too thick to allow the sides of the frame to be spread apart wide enough for these fingers to slip into place easily. They must be filed down before they can be inserted.

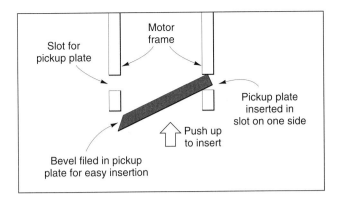

Slot for pickup plate

Motor frame

Pickup plate inserted in slot on one side

Push up to insert

Bevel filed in pickup plate for easy insertion

It is necessary to file the fingers on only *one* side. Shape them in a beveled pattern as shown in the diagram, and leave only enough material to ensure that they will not slip out of the frame. Before inserting the bracket, be sure that you solder the internal wire from the motor to the inside of the metal pickup roller frame.

With this done, insert the unaltered fingers in one side of the frame. Then use a large screwdriver to spread the frame slightly and press the beveled side of the fiber bracket down into place. This bracket is fairly flexible and will bend enough to slide easily into position. Make sure the fingers go into the slots in the motor frame.

A little practice is required to make a neat installation, but after you have replaced a few of them (or a couple of hundred, as I have), a perfect repair is possible in a very short time.

29 Optional Catenary Operation

Lionel locomotives equipped with metal pantographs, such as the big rectifier electrics, EP-5 and GG-1 models, can be altered to receive current from overhead wires rather than from the third-rail pickup rollers. The power wire from the motor is disconnected from the third-rail pickup plate; it is then resoldered to the mounting tab beneath the pantograph inside the locomotive cab, as shown in the photo below.

However, rerouting the wire in this manner limits the locomotive exclusively to catenary operation, whereas it might be desirable to be able to run the unit in locations without overhead lines or on other hobbyists' layouts. One could connect the motor to both the pantograph and the third-rail pickup, but this defeats the purpose of overhead operation.

An electric-style locomotive operating exclusively from overhead lines can be controlled independently of other locos on the same trackage. For example, if throttle A of a ZW transformer is wired to the third rail and throttle D is connected to the overhead wire, the speed, direction and sound mechanisms (horn, whistle) of each locomotive can be operated independently of the other.

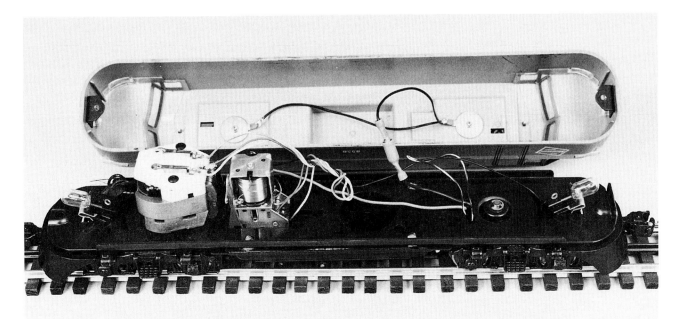

It is desirable, therefore, to provide a quick and convenient method to switch back and forth between third rail and catenary operation. The easiest way to accomplish this is to install a miniature SPDT (single pole, double throw) toggle switch, as shown in the photo below. The center pole of the switch is soldered to the motor wire, one of the outer poles is connected to the pantograph, and the other is wired to the third-rail pickup. One position of the toggle switch directs current from the third rail to the motor, while throwing the toggle in the opposite direction connects the pantograph instead.

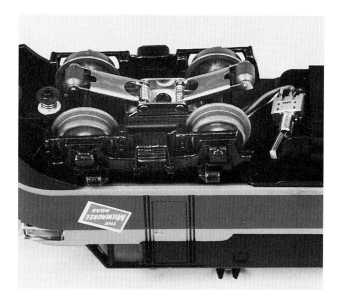

Although the undersides of various Lionel locomotive frames differ, it should be possible to route the wires in such a manner that the toggle switch is easily accessible, as shown in the photo above. It may be mounted permanently by drilling a hole in the engine's frame and screwing it in place, but this alteration should not be necessary. If stiff, heavy gauge wire is used for both the third-rail and the motor connections, the wire can be bent to shape in such a way as to keep the toggle switch in place without extra support. However, the wire that leads to the pantograph should be of the highly flexible, stranded variety and should be somewhat longer than necessary to reach the pantograph connection. This allows the cab to be removed easily for servicing.

30 Running DC Motors with AC Transformers

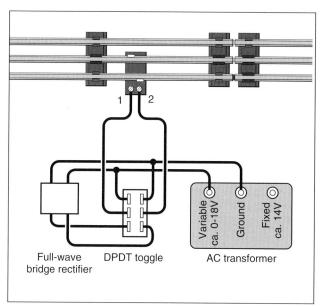

Full-wave bridge rectifier   DPDT toggle   AC transformer

The locomotives in some inexpensive Lionel train sets produced during the modern era (1970 to the present) come equipped with low-cost DC (direct current) can motors, rather than the familiar universal motor that powers all postwar and most modern era Lionel locomotives. These units are supplied with their own DC transformers and cannot be operated with transformers producing alternating current (AC). Unfortunately for DC-set owners, the vast majority of toy train transformers made by Lionel, Marx, and American Flyer are AC.

It is possible to connect an AC transformer to the track through a DPDT switch connected to a full-wave bridge rectifier. There are six contacts on the DPDT switch, and the wires should be attached as shown above. Use at least a 50-volt rectifier and a knife DPDT, or a toggle rated at 5 amps or more.

When thrown in one direction, the switch sends AC current to the track. This setting should be used for Lionel locomotives (the vast majority) with universal AC motors. In the opposite position, the DPDT routes the current through the rectifier and supplies DC current instead. Use this setting when running your locomotives with DC can motors on the layout.

Note that locomotives with universal motors will also run on the DC current, and at slightly faster speeds than on AC. However, those with relay-activated whistles cannot be used, as the whistle motors will run all the time if the train is operated on DC. *Never* operate DC can motors on AC current; it can permanently damage them.

31 Alternate Track Power

A simple DPDT switch will allow you to wire two different transformers to the same layout and select one or the other with ease. The diagram shows the wiring pattern. The most obvious use of this circuit is to have the option of either an AC or a DC transformer, to allow you to run the two types of modern era Lionel locomotives (see previous entry, "Running DC Motors With AC Transformers").

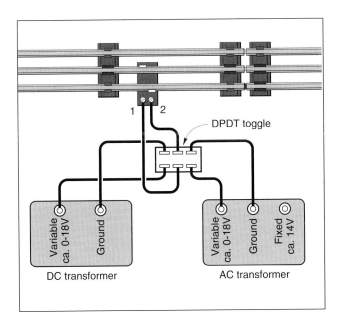

DC transformer   AC transformer

Operators who use transformers with high- and low-speed ranges connected to the rheostat (R or 1033, for example) can also benefit from this circuit. Connect the high-voltage range to one side of the DPDT and the low range to the other, and you can select either range with the switch. If the locomotive in use

draws a large amount of current, such as a Lionel 263E, select the high range. When running smaller engines, such as those supplied with the prewar O-27 sets and smaller postwar trains such as Scouts, choose the low range.

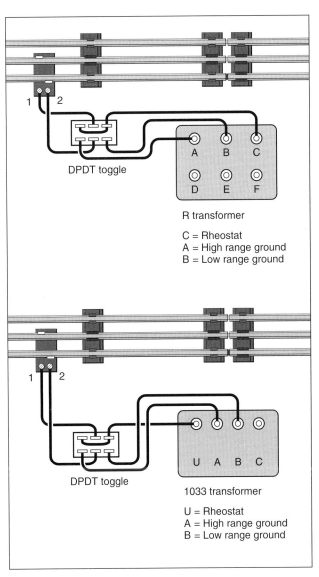

DPDT toggle

R transformer

C = Rheostat
A = High range ground
B = Low range ground

DPDT toggle

1033 transformer

U = Rheostat
A = High range ground
B = Low range ground

The diagram illustrates (at top) the connections used for a Lionel Type "R" transformer, which has two voltage ranges available from a single rheostat: 6 to 16 volts and 14 to 24 volts. Below are the connections for a 1033 transformer, which has both 0- to 11-volt and 5- to 16-volt variable circuits on the rheostat speed control.

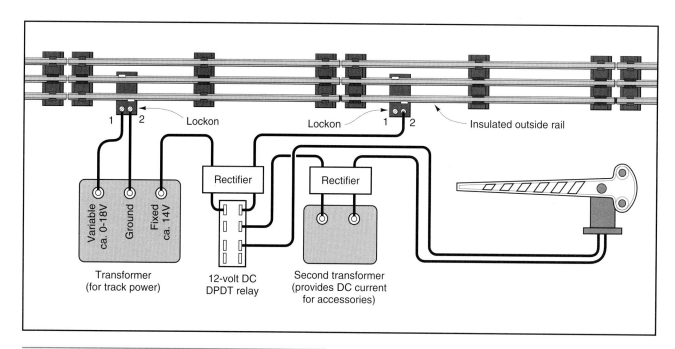

Transformer (for track power) — Variable ca. 0-18V | Ground | Fixed ca. 14V

12-volt DC DPDT relay

Second transformer (provides DC current for accessories)

Lockon — 1 2 — Lockon — 1 2 — Insulated outside rail

Rectifier — Rectifier

32 Silencing Solenoid Accessories

Lionel's solenoid-triggered accessories, such as crossing gates, semaphores, and the ubiquitous gateman, have an annoying tendency to buzz when in operation. They also frequently slow down a passing train by siphoning off current from the track. There's an easy way to quiet them completely and at the same time maintain train speed.

The key is to give them an independent power source that provides DC current instead of the AC from a standard toy train transformer. If you use pressure contactors under the track, the cost of this system is minimal, but if you use insulated running rails to trigger your accessories, you'll have to invest a few bucks in relays and rectifiers. However, if the buzzing solenoids drive you as crazy as they do me, the result is well worth the effort and expense.

You will need an AC relay, or a DC relay with a full-wave bridge rectifier, that operates on one of the fixed voltages available from a Lionel transformer. A 12-volt relay can be connected to a fixed-voltage post of about 9 to 15 volts. A 24-volt relay operates easily on the 20 volts supplied by post D on a KW transformer, or post B or C on a ZW, turned up to the highest setting.

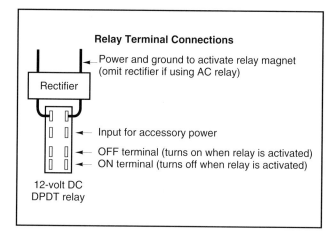

Relay Terminal Connections

Power and ground to activate relay magnet (omit rectifier if using AC relay)

Rectifier

Input for accessory power

OFF terminal (turns on when relay is activated)

ON terminal (turns off when relay is activated)

12-volt DC DPDT relay

Connect the crossing gate or similar accessory as shown in the diagram at the top of the page. The DC current that powers the accessory should be supplied by a separate small Lionel transformer, as shown. Use the posts that normally supply track power, so you can use the speed control handle to govern the amount of current reaching the accessory. That way you can control how fast the gate comes down, the semaphore arm descends, etc. Using a second transformer in this way ensures that train speed will be unaffected by the operation of the accessory.

33 Wipers for Positive Ground

Before Christmas my wife picked up a new-in-the-box Lionel James Gang set, manufactured in 1979, and we set it up to run around the tree. Much to our chagrin, the locomotive ran erratically. A trip to the test bench soon showed why. The motor ran fine with one of the transformer leads connected to the middle rail shoe and the other clipped to the metal frame. But if I moved the second lead from the frame to the rim of a driving wheel, the motor hardly turned.

The James Gang locomotive is a very lightweight version of the *General* style first introduced in 1957. It has a DC can motor and plastic-centered wheels with metal rims. Since 1980, the rims had developed a film of oxidation that prevented current from traveling through them to the track, thus creating a faulty ground.

The first step was to clean the wheel rims with a mild abrasive; I used very fine emery paper. This resulted is slightly improved performance, but the locomotive still ran in fits and starts, symptomatic of a continuing poor ground connection through the drive wheels. Since the ground is transmitted from the rails through the wheels, then through the frame to the motor, it was apparent that a more positive connection was needed.

The solution was easy. I fashioned a small wiper from flexible brass stock and mounted it under a screw on the frame, as shown in the photo (below left). The free end of the wiper rubs against the metal rim of the drive wheel, thus providing a more constant, positive, and secure ground. The little *General* now performs as reliably as its heavier cousins and makes a fine display under the Christmas tree.

34 TV Tuner Spray

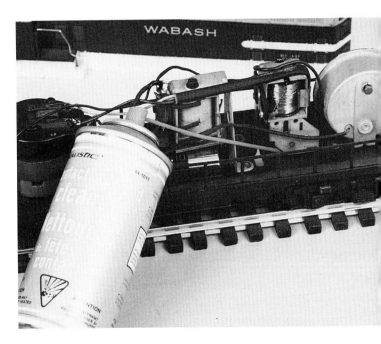

Any TV dealer or repair shop will sell you a small spray can of a cleaner designed for the contacts on tuner controls. The can comes with a thin plastic spout that allows you to direct the spray into tight places. This product sprays on wet, but dries almost instantly, greatly improving the conduction of electricity, even through dirty or oxidized surfaces. It's ideal for hard-to-clean areas, such as E-unit drums. If you operate prewar Lionel trains with the old and notoriously troublesome pendulum reverse units, you may find this spray to be the perfect answer to more reliable operation.

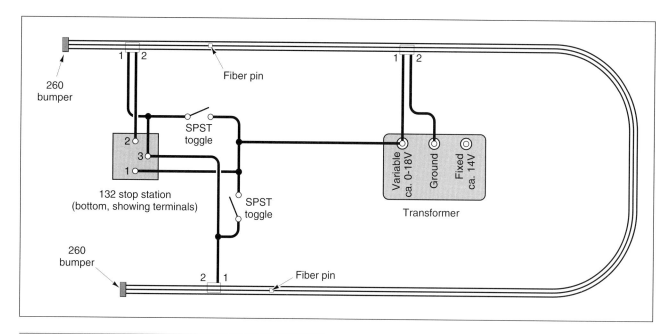

Fiber pin

260 bumper

1 2

2
3
1

SPST toggle

132 stop station
(bottom, showing terminals)

SPST toggle

260 bumper

2 1

Fiber pin

1 2

Variable ca. 0-18V   Ground   Fixed ca. 14V

Transformer

35 Automatic Point-to-Point Commuter Line

All you need for this lively addition to your layout is an automatic stop station such as Lionel's No. 132, a Budd Rail Diesel Car (RDC), and a stretch of track that is isolated from the rest of your layout. Since RDCs were designed for commuter service, a point-to-point line between two towns or cities would be ideal.

At each end of the line, provide a length of track with the middle rail insulated, and wire it to the transformer through the 132 stop station as shown in the diagram. Use at least two and preferably three lengths of track for these insulated sections, with bumpers (Lionel's no. 260, for example) at the end.

One stop station is sufficient, but you can use a different one at each end of the line if you wish. Note that the insulated sections are also provided with a direct wiring connection through a toggle switch. This allows the operator to bypass the automatic stop circuit for manual control.

In automatic operation, the Budd car leaves one station and travels to the opposite end, where the stop circuit cuts off its current, causing it to stop. When the circuit kicks in again, the train's E-unit comes on in neutral. After a few seconds, the stop circuit disconnects power again, then comes on again after a short pause. This time the E-unit cycles to reverse, and the Budd car proceeds to the opposite station, where the whole process repeats itself.

The rail diesel car will travel back and forth as long as the power is on, stopping briefly at each end to discharge passengers, without any intervention from the operator. If you want to deviate from this pattern, flip the toggle that sends current to the ends of the track; you can then control the Budd car manually from the transformer.

36 Automatic Point-to-Point Trolley Line

This variation on tip no. 35 will allow a Lionel no. 60 trolley, or one of the modern era reissues, to travel back and forth automatically. Wire it exactly as shown above, but use only *one* section of track for each of the insulated sections at the ends.

Also be sure the no. 260 bumpers are fastened tightly to the track, as explained in Chapter One under the heading "Secure Mounting of Lionel Bumpers." This is essential, since the trolley reverse mechanism is triggered by firm contact with the bumper.

The stop station circuit stops the trolley, just

like the Budd car in the previous entry. If the trolley is moving slowly, it will stop before reaching the bumper. When the circuit turns track power back on, the trolley continues in the same direction toward the bumper, reverses itself, and heads off in the opposite direction. If it is traveling at high speed, the trolley may coast all the way to the bumper before stopping. Then, it will already be in reverse mode when the circuit turns on again.

If two or three sections of insulated track are provided, as with the Budd cars, the trolley will still work, but it cannot coast as far as the bumper. As soon as power is restored by the stop station circuit, the trolley will continue to the bumper and reverse itself. However, the circuit may turn off again before the trolley clears the insulated section. This is no problem; when power comes on again after a few seconds, it will continue on its way. But this provides a double stop at the station, which is not as realistic.

37 Trolley Line with Intermediate Stops

Another variation on the preceding circuit is ideal for a large layout with several towns or cities. The circuit allows a trolley to travel from town to town, stopping briefly at each one; only one stop circuit is required. The diagram below shows how to wire it.

38 Automatic Circuit for Two Trolleys

James Campbell of Staten Island, New York, sent me a design for automatic control of two trolleys (page 30). The double main line ends in a pair of automatic nonderailing Lionel switches, such as the postwar no. 1122 or 022, or the modern era equivalents.

The trolleys start at opposite ends simultaneously. The switches are set at the beginning so one trolley goes down the straight track and the other takes the passing siding. Each continues to the far end, where it reverses at the bumper. Thanks to the nonderailing switches, each trolley will automatically select the same route for the return trip, passing each other in the middle.

Mr. Campbell was having a problem with the layout, however, which is why he wrote to me. One of his trolleys ran faster and eventually caught up with the other one, causing a collision. He asked if a relay could be used to slow down the faster trolley when it begins to overtake the slower one.

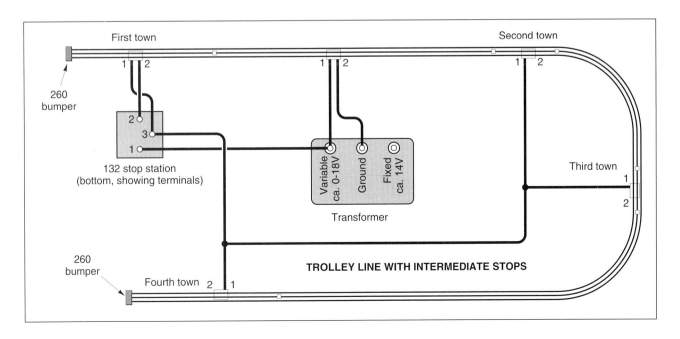

TROLLEY LINE WITH INTERMEDIATE STOPS

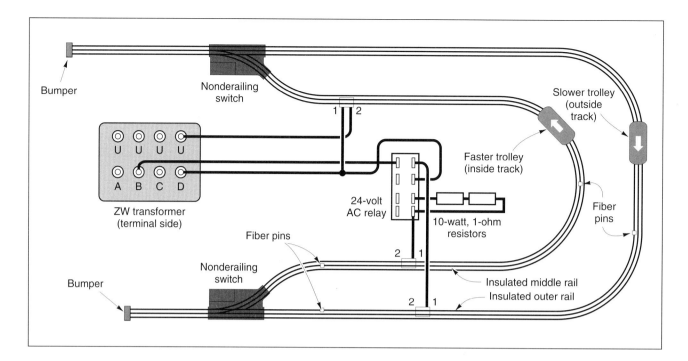

Bumper
Nonderailing switch
1 2
ZW transformer (terminal side)
U U U U
A B C D
24-volt AC relay
10-watt, 1-ohm resistors
Slower trolley (outside track)
Faster trolley (inside track)
Fiber pins
Fiber pins
Nonderailing switch
Bumper
2 1
2 1
Insulated middle rail
Insulated outer rail

The diagram above shows the wiring involved. The faster trolley is assigned to the passing siding, and a length of track (three to five sections) is isolated with fiber pins in the middle rail.

On the main line, a similar length of track is provided with an insulated *outside* rail, as described in Chapter One under the heading "Making Insulated Track Sections." Alternatively, you can buy such sections ready-made from Lionel or K-Line.

As the faster trolley begins to catch up with the slower one, eventually it will be in the section with the insulated middle rail at the same time the slower one is in the insulated outside rail section. This causes the relay to trip and reduces the amount of current that reaches the faster trolley, slowing it down.

The amount the trolley slows down depends upon how many resistors are wired to the relay. One 10-watt, 1-ohm resistor will slow it slightly; two will slow it quite a bit. Or the resistor can be omitted entirely, and the faster trolley will stop until the slower one leaves the insulated-outside-rail section. Then the relay will turn off, and current will be restored to the faster trolley.

The circuit shows a 24-volt alternating current (AC) DPDT relay connected to an accessory post (B) of a ZW transformer turned to

its highest setting, producing about 20 volts. The KW transformer also has a 20-volt fixed-voltage post. If you have a smaller transformer, you can use a 12-volt relay instead, which will work on any fixed-voltage post producing between 9 and 15 volts. Be sure the relay is for AC current; if you use a direct current (DC) relay, equip it with a full-wave bridge rectifier, as explained in Chapter Four under the heading "Using DC Relays With Lionel AC Transformers."

39 Simplified Automatic Circuit for Two Trolleys

There's an easier, less expensive way to regulate the speed of a faster trolley, provided you have a transformer with two throttles, such as a ZW or a KW. The circuit is shown in the diagram on page 31. However, this solution is less positive than the relay-activated one described above.

One throttle is wired to the main line and the two end sections, and is set for the speed desired for the slower-running trolley. The passing siding is isolated at each end with fiber pins in the middle rail and is wired to the second throttle. This throttle is set to slightly

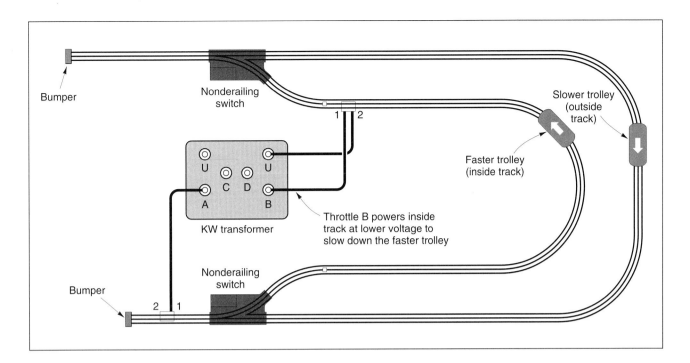

Bumper

Nonderailing switch

1 2

KW transformer

U U
C D
A B

Throttle B powers inside track at lower voltage to slow down the faster trolley

Bumper

Nonderailing switch

2 1

Slower trolley (outside track)

Faster trolley (inside track)

less voltage, adjusted so that the faster trolley is slowed down to approximately the same speed as the slower one.

Depending upon how carefully the throttles are adjusted, this circuit will keep the two trolleys in balance for a longer period. However, it will be difficult to achieve a precise balance between the two throttles; eventually one will get too close to the other, so you'll want to check them periodically.

Chapter Three

ILLUMINATION IDEAS

*L*ights bring a train layout to life. Without the warmth of glowing windows and streetlights, the towns seem barren and lifeless. Without the beam of its headlight, a locomotive loses much of its romance. The red and green lenses of switch controllers and block signals add color and interest to an otherwise lifeless scene. Here are some ideas to use light to best advantage.

> **Warning:** A few projects described in this and succeeding chapters involve 115-VAC wiring. These connections must be made properly to avoid the possibility of a dangerous, potentially fatal, electrical shock. Those unfamiliar with 115-VAC wiring should not attempt these projects without consulting a professional electrician.

40 Lighted Locomotive Cabs

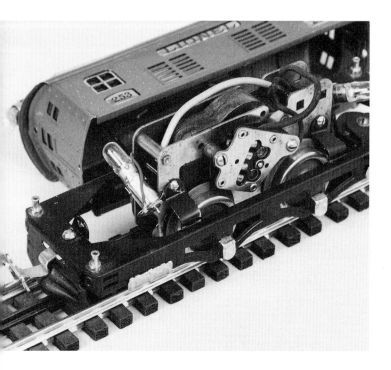

Adding an interior light to locomotives, such as Lionel's NW-2 switchers or prewar boxcab electrics, is easy to do and adds interest to the engines. Very few parts are needed: a 14-volt bulb (either screw or bayonet base); a matching socket with wiring tabs; a miniature nut, bolt, and washer; and a short length of wire.

The wiring tabs of most sockets have one or two small holes punched in them. One tab is in contact with the wall of the socket itself and is the ground connection. The other tab is fastened to the center of the socket base and is separated from the wall by an insulating washer.

Mount the motor frame's ground tab at any convenient location, making sure to leave enough clearance for the socket and bulb when the body of the locomotive is replaced. Enlarge the hole in the mounting tab with an awl until it is large enough for the miniature bolt to pass through. Find an unused hole on the motor frame, and bolt it on with the nut and washer.

If there is no hole in the frame in a convenient location, you might be able to slip the tab between the frame and the brushplate, or between the frame and the E-unit. Anywhere is fine, as long as the light from the bulb will be visible when the cab is back on and as long as it doesn't interfere with the mechanism in any way. If necessary, solder a length of strip brass or stiff wire to the ground tab to make an extension to hold the bulb in place.

Solder a short length of wire to the other tab and then to the nearest available hot wire. Usually the most convenient spot for this hookup is the locomotive's headlight wire. On prewar locomotives with a manual reverse, attach it to the screw post wire on the reverse switch that connects to the third-rail pickup plate. Before reassembling the locomotive, test the motor on a track to be sure the bulb lights. Now your miniature crew can see to operate the brakes and throttle.

41 Adding Locomotive Headlights

Some of Lionel's lower priced locomotives and the various small motorized units, such as the no. 41 Army Switcher, came without operating headlights. Miniature screw bulbs and sockets can rectify this problem.

Connections are made in the same manner as described above under "Lighted Locomotive Cabs." The only differences are the size of the bulbs and the provision of a barrier to prevent possible damage to the plastic shell from the bulb's heat. This barrier is a simple square of aluminum foil, cut and folded to fit inside the body shell. For the rear-facing light in the Canadian Pacific snowplow shown in the photo, the bulb must be placed very close to the roof of the cab. The aluminum foil lining the inside of the roof lessens the heat

transfer and also reflects light back into the interior of the cab.

42 Window Glazing

Compare the two prewar boxcab locomotives in the photograph below. Interior cab lights look much better with a lightly frosted

window material installed to diffuse the light, as in the model at left. While the better postwar and modern era diesels have plastic in the windows, some lack glazing and can also benefit from this technique.

Frosted glazing material is available from most toy train parts suppliers or can be made from plastic sheets purchased at a stationery store. Cut the panes slightly oversize. On locomotives with separate window frames, cut slots in the pane to match the positions of the mounting tabs, and reinstall the frame and pane together. If the window frames are an integral part of the cab sides, tape the panes in place. Use short strips of premium transparent tape such as Scotch Brand Magic Tape. Cheaper transparent tape should not be used, as it will dry up and crack; it will also leave a nasty residue on the inside of the window frames. The premium tape can be removed at any time without a trace.

This same technique is especially effective when used with prewar Lionel bungalows. Most of these little houses came with a single bare bulb inside, lighting them up with a definite "hot spot." By glazing the windows with

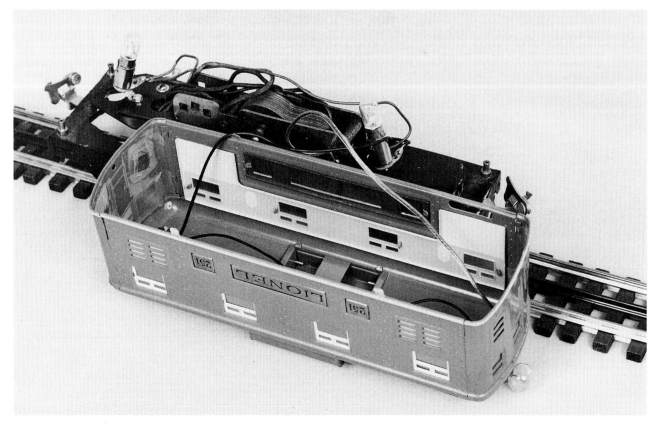

a slightly frosted material, the overall illumination is spread more evenly throughout the building, resulting in a much more pleasing appearance.

Plasticville buildings look better when their windows are glazed, even if the interiors are not lighted. It's easy to light one of these structures, however, with a socket and a 14-volt bulb. The socket need not be attached to the house, but can be mounted on the layout surface, with the house simply placed over it.

43 Industrial Lighting

Some buildings on your layout look best with amber bulbs installed inside instead of clear ones. For example, a subdued amber glow looks just right in a Lionel no. 435 or 436 Power Station or in the lower story of a no. 437 Switch Signal Tower.

The power stations have no sockets for interior lighting because they were originally intended to cover a transformer. However, since the middle of the base is cut out for the transformer, it is easy to install a light. The best way to light a power station is to screw a plastic-framed screw socket directly to the layout table. Changing the bulb is easy—just lift up the building for access.

44 Quick and Easy Lampposts

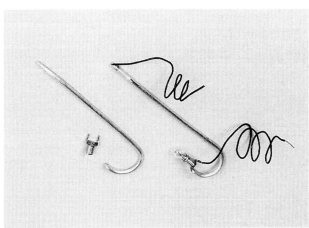

A layout can be made to look larger by locating smaller accessories at the back and larger ones up front. This forces the illusion of perspective. One of the most effective methods of achieving this is to make a series of small lampposts to line a distant street. Lionel lampposts are large and look good in the foreground; the contrast with smaller versions makes the back of the layout seem much farther away and the layout bigger. The small lampposts are easily made from ¼" aluminum ground cable, miniature screw-type sockets, and miniature bulbs.

Cut the ground cable to length and curve it at one end to make a gooseneck lamp standard. Flatten the end as shown in the photo above, and drill a small hole in the end. Most miniature sockets have two small tabs attached, one of which is a ground (connected to the wall of the socket) and the other a hot wire connection (through the insulated washer in the center of the socket base).

Bend the ground tab and insert it through the drilled hole, then bend it over tightly with pliers. Because the lamppost is made from aluminum, it is not possible to solder this tab in place, so you must crimp it tightly.

Solder a very thin wire to the other tab. Drill a ¼" hole in the tabletop and insert the lamp; then drill a small hole next to it for the hot wire. Connect this wire to the transformer's hot post, and run a lead from the ground post, wrapping it around the base of the post where it protrudes beneath the layout. Wire a toggle switch on the control panel into the hot line so you can turn the lamp on and off.

These lamps are crude and do not stand up well to close inspection, but they are convincing when located at a distance from the viewer, especially in a string of six or eight. Multiple lamps may be wired together in parallel. Placed along a city street, they present a very pleasing appearance and shed a gentle light on nearby models and scenic details.

45 Telegraph Pole Streetlights

Miniature bulbs and sockets make convincing hanging lamps when installed on telegraph poles. Curve a short length of copper wire to

the shape shown in the photo below left. Solder one end to the middle terminal of the miniature socket. For this application, use sockets *without* solder tabs. This type of socket has a tiny brass eyelet in the center of the insulated base. Insert the end of the wire into the eyelet and solder in place.

Drill a hole through the telegraph pole beneath the crossarms and insert the other end of the wire. Adjust the bend in the wire to hold the bulb in the proper position. Solder a very thin wire (one strand taken from multiple-stranded hookup wire) to the hanger and another to the casing of the socket. These form the hot and ground connections. They may be connected to wires beneath the base of the layout, but a more realistic method is to use wires between the telegraph poles to power them. This is shown in the photo and is explained more fully under the heading "Functional Telegraph Pole Wiring" in Chapter Four.

46 Firebox Illumination

Large prewar O gauge locomotives, such as Lionel's nos. 260 and 263, and American Flyer's 3316 type, have a red bulb mounted below the cab to simulate the glow of a steam

engine's firebox. (Although this feature was dropped from Lionel's postwar trains, some modern era locomotives are now appearing with lighted fireboxes.) This feature is also found on many Standard gauge locomotives. If you are interested in this feature, you will be pleased to know that it is possible to mount a socket in most smaller locomotives.

A miniature socket and bulb combination works best, as there is often very little clearance above the trailing truck, but in some models (such as Lionel's no. 262 as shown) a larger bulb can be used. Each locomotive is different, and a means will have to be found for mounting the bulb. In the 262, the ground tab of the socket was fastened to the frame by one of the cab mounting bolts. The hot wire was spliced into the headlight circuit.

47 Extra Lights for Larger Buildings and Cars

Some Lionel buildings, such as the large no. 124 Station, are inadequately lit. It is possible to improve the interior illumination by increasing the voltage to (or above) the recommended maximum for the bulb, but this shortens its life and makes the lighting seem somewhat harsh. It's better to add one or two more bulbs. The same trick works with large passenger cars, such as Lionel's 710 series and the biggest Ives coaches.

All you need is a socket, bulb, and some stiff wire for each additional bulb. Stiff wire is preferable, since it can be used as a support for the socket, as shown inside the station in the photo below.

Solder two wires to the socket, one to each terminal tab, and connect them to the ground and power connections inside the station. Bend the wires until the socket is where you want it, screw in a bulb, and see how much better it looks with two or three bulbs instead of only one.

48 Sensitive Crossing Flasher Circuit

The circuit in Lionel's big no. 79 Highway Flasher (prewar) is operated by a bimetallic strip that alternately heats and cools to open and close a set of momentary contacts. This circuit is highly sensitive to the voltage input and the load of each bulb. To achieve an even alternation between the two bulbs, a little experimentation is needed; there seems to be considerable variation between different examples of this accessory.

The one shown in the picture operates best at very low voltage. At about 6 volts, the circuit heats and cools at an even rate, causing each bulb to flash for about the same length of time. Increasing the voltage makes the bimetallic strip heat more quickly and stay open longer, thus making one bulb flash for a much longer time than the other.

You might think that installing two identical 6-volt bulbs would make the accessory work well, but this is not the case. Although the rate of flash is even, one bulb shines more brightly than the other.

To solve this problem, I experimented with bulbs having varying load requirements and finally found two that work well together. One is a 6-volt smoke detector bulb, and the other is from a generator-type bicycle headlight. One draws about 200 milliamps, while the other is rated at about 230.

By putting the higher-rated lamp in the side of the circuit that shines more brightly, the extra current draw balances the circuit. Now my no. 79 flashes evenly, both in brightness and in regularity.

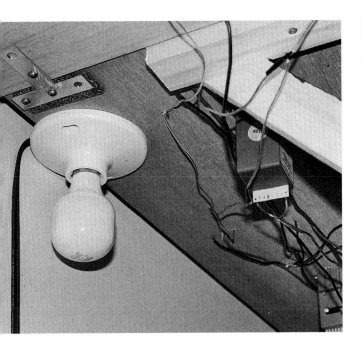

49 Under-the-Table Lighting

This idea seems too obvious to include, but I am amazed at how many modelers have failed to use it. Crawling around beneath a layout is often awkward, and visibility is generally not very good. Room lights seldom reach the underside of the layout, and it can be awkward and inconvenient to depend upon a portable lamp for illumination. In addition, a lamp sitting on the floor is often in the way and is easily kicked over. Besides, its low angle is not always suitable for seeing one's work clearly.

Why not mount one or more lights permanently under the table? Inexpensive sockets are available at the hardware store, as are lamp cord and wall plugs. Another approach is to buy an extension cord, cut off the end opposite the wall plug, and connect each of the two wires to one of the screw terminals of the socket.

A chain pull on the socket makes it easy to turn on and off from under the layout, or you can wire it through a toggle switch on the control panel. Two, three, or even more bulbs may be wired in parallel for large layouts. If you mount the sockets at a high level, they will be out of the way and spread light from above your work.

50 Entry Lights

Adding little touches can make a good layout a great one! One of the most common additions is a light fixture beside the doorway of a home, and it's easy to add. Very small 12-volt bulbs with tiny cylindrical bases are available from electronic supply stores. These bulbs have two wire pins, which serve as electrical contacts, extending from the base. The base itself is a reasonable approximation of an outdoor light fixture.

Using a subminiature bit, drill two holes into the door frame at the side of or above the doorway, and insert the bulb. If you use a small enough drill, the pins will hold the bulb in place by friction. Alternatively, a tiny dot of cement will keep the bulb in place. Run a pair of wires from the ground and hot connections of the building's interior light, and solder them to the pins. The outside light will now come on whenever the inside of the house is illuminated. You could also run a separate circuit to the outside light, so it may be left on when the building itself is dark.

Though this installation is relatively permanent, in that it requires unsoldering if the bulb needs replacing, it is advisable to use lower voltage in this circuit, approximately 10 volts for a 12-volt bulb. This not only ensures long life, it also looks more realistic to have a soft glow rather than a bright point of light beside an entrance. In fact, most toy train layouts look better with slightly reduced lighting intensity in all buildings and lampposts. When operated this way, the bulbs will last almost indefinitely.

51 Level of Illumination

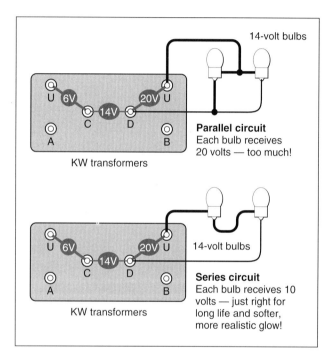

Parallel circuit
Each bulb receives 20 volts — too much!

KW transformers

Series circuit
Each bulb receives 10 volts — just right for long life and softer, more realistic glow!

KW transformers

14-volt bulbs

Except for the most inexpensive models, Lionel transformers provide fixed-voltage circuits for the operation of accessories. On the big ZW model, there are two adjustable circuits that can be set to any level up to about 21 volts. The bulbs in most Lionel accessories, such as signals, buildings and lampposts, are rated at 14 volts. Some transformers provide a 14-volt circuit, and the ZW can be set at this level, but that is not necessarily the best choice. Operating these bulbs at their full rating shortens their life considerably, and their brightness is somewhat unrealistic.

Instead, choose a circuit that provides approximately 10 or 11 volts, as can be obtained from a Lionel model no. 1033 transformer.

This reduced power greatly increases bulb life, and the softer glow is more pleasant and more realistic.

Sometimes it will take a little ingenuity to find a circuit that will satisfy these requirements. For example, Lionel's KW transformer has three fixed voltages: 6, 14, and 20. There is no provision for 11 volts, such as that provided by the 1033. Nevertheless, it is not difficult to get a 10-volt circuit by wiring two bulbs in series, rather than parallel. The diagram shows how to wire them. When connected in this fashion, each bulb draws only 10 volts from the 20-volt circuit. A 14-volt bulb operating on 10 volts looks fine.

Each of Lionel's most popular transformers has its own peculiar pattern of fixed-voltage circuits. Sometimes the best solution is to use bulbs with lower or higher ratings. For example, substituting 18-volt bulbs for the 14-volt type, and connecting them to the 14-volt terminals of a KW transformer, achieves about the same result as running 14-volt bulbs on 10 volts. The KW also has a 6-volt circuit, which can be used to power 8-volt bulbs with longer life and a softer glow. Analyze the situation created by your own equipment, then devise a combination of fixed voltages and bulb ratings to provide the desired results.

52 Table Lamps (or Candles) in Your Diner

Another small but significant detail that adds charm to a layout is the provision of individual table lamps in the windows of a diner. In larger models, such as Lionel's prewar no. 442 shown in the photo on page 41, miniature screw-base bulbs are ideal. A series of sockets, in this case eight, is connected in a string by stiff wire, which makes the lights easy to position and ensures they will stay in place. To give a soft illumination, I used a 6-volt fixed-voltage post.

In smaller diners, grain-of-wheat bulbs look best. These do not require sockets, so I suggest mounting them on a piece of stripwood.

The local beanery acquires a certain ambience once lamps are placed on the tables.

Position the bulbs so that when viewed from outside, they appear to be resting on tables at the level of the bottom of the window frames.

53 Transformer Pilot Light

Some Lionel transformers have no pilot lights, and since they have no on-off switches either, it's easy to forget to turn them off after use. May I suggest a pilot light?

Just wire a socket and bulb (red is a logical choice) to a fixed-voltage post, and locate it on the control panel. Be sure to choose a bulb of the proper voltage for the fixed-voltage post you elect to use. A 6-volt bulb connected to the 6-volt post of a KW transformer, for example, works just fine.

54 Scenic Transformer Pilot Light

On the layout I have in my office at Acadia University, I have the transformer located in a no. 435 Power Station, exactly as Lionel intended this accessory to be used. However, instead of locating the pilot light on the control panel, I mounted it directly on the transformer inside the Power Station. It now does double duty: it illuminates the building, and it serves as a reminder to me to turn off the current when I'm finished running the trains.

Chapter Four

WIRING WIZARDRY

*G*ood *wiring is essential to good operation. It should be effi-cient, foolproof, flexible, convenient, and most of all, in-visible. Many hobbyists are intimidated by wiring, but there's not that much to it, especially if you approach it one wire at a time. The tips that follow will help you achieve good operation.*

55 Quick and Easy Control Panel

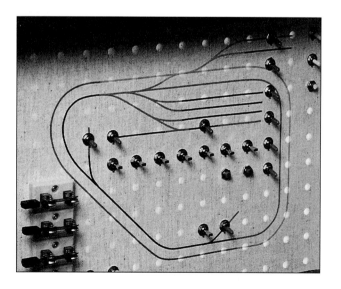

One of the most time-consuming tasks in building a control panel is planning the location of the various switches and drilling holes

for them. The method described here elimi-nates drilling completely and allows you to add switches at any point or time without marring the surface of the panel.

Build the panel from an appropriately sized rectangle of pegboard with ¼" holes. Cover the surface with self-adhesive vinyl contact paper, then place a light behind the panel, as shown in the photo. This will let you see the location of all the holes.

Draw your track plan on the surface of the contact paper, or use flexible artist's tape, available in a variety of widths and colors from art supply stores. I've found the ¹⁄₁₆" size easiest to work with.

Once you decide where the block control switches and turnout controls will be, cut out the appropriate hole in the contact paper, in-sert a miniature toggle switch with a ¼" neck, and wire it up. You can add a switch to the panel quickly and easily at any time without drilling, and the panel looks nice at any stage

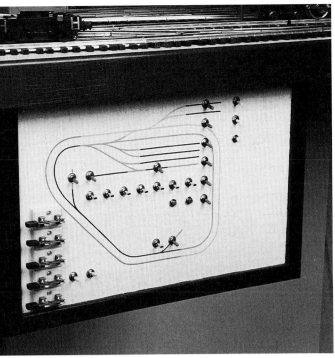

are in Chapter One, under the heading "Toggle Controls for Lionel Switches."

56 Recessed Control Panel

Toggle switches that protrude from a control panel can be annoying in close quarters and are always subject to damage. Recessing these toggles is easy, however.

Locate the control panel on a ¾"-thick board (the framework of our portable layout was used here). With a keyhole saw or electric jigsaw, cut out appropriately sized rectangles. Mount vinyl-covered pieces of pegboard behind the cutouts, as shown in the photo directly below, and install the toggle switches and pushbuttons, as described in tip no. 55.

For a neat appearance, line the cutout areas with the same adhesive vinyl contact paper used to cover the pegboard. The result is pleasing to the eye, convenient to the hand during operation, and protected from accidental damage from passersby.

of construction. Without back lighting, the unused holes are not visible, as shown in the photo above.

Miniature toggle switches and pushbuttons are made in many different configurations and may be substituted for such Lionel items as switch controllers and remote control boxes. Since the Lionel versions are big and bulky, and take up a lot of room on a control panel, using these small substitutes is desirable. In addition, they allow you to locate the control at the proper place on the track plan diagram for easy recognition while operating. The wiring diagrams for track-related controls

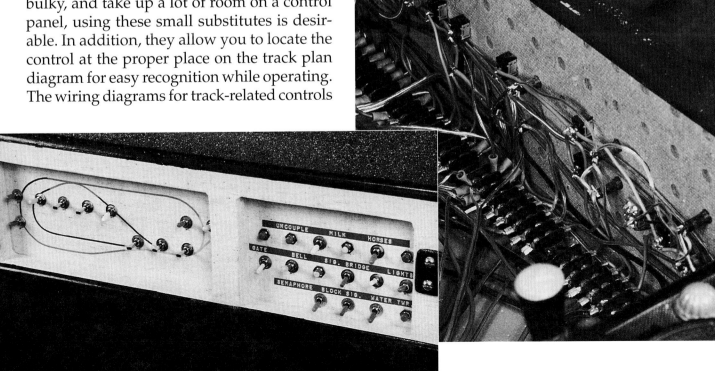

57 Solderless Wiring Connections

Using a soldering iron or gun overhead while lying on one's back under a layout is not much fun. Besides the danger of dripping hot solder on clothes or skin, the task is awkward and the results are too permanent. When changes or repairs are required, wires must either be unsoldered or cut. There's an easier way.

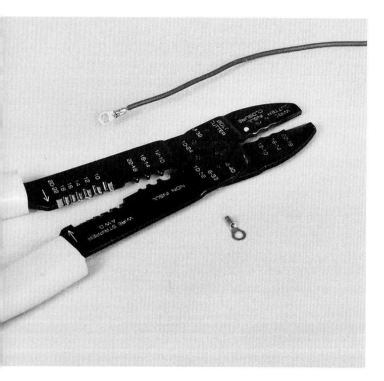

For every track block or accessory on the layout, run short lengths of wire from their terminals through holes in the tabletop, extending just a couple of inches below the table. Strip about ¼" of insulation from the ends of these wires. Cut the longer leads from the control panel to reach these short leads, but don't solder them. Instead, crimp a solderless lug on the end of the wire, as shown in the top photo at left.

Put a very short (⅜" by #4) self-tapping screw through the hole in the lug, and screw it into the underside of the tabletop, with the end of the lead from the accessory or track under the lug. Tighten the screw, and the pressure will ensure a firm, positive electrical connection. The whole operation takes half the time required for soldering a connection, and moving the accessory at a later date is as easy as unscrewing the lug.

58 Quick-disconnect Plugs and Sockets

In some situations, it is desirable to be able to connect and disconnect wiring from accessories. For example, on the portable layout my wife and I take to train shows and schools, the taller accessories are removable for transport. It would take a lot longer to set up this display if we had to fasten all the wiring to terminal strips.

As described under the heading "Supplementary Pickups" in Chapter Two, some of our locomotives are equipped with jumper wires between the motor and the pickup roller in the whistle tender or the first lighted passenger car. It is essential that these connections be easily separated when the trains are moved to and from the track.

Quick-disconnect plugs and sockets are available from electronics and auto supply stores in a variety of sizes for different gauges of wire. The smallest are best for most model railroad applications. They are solderless, being attached with a crimping tool. The simplest type (shown in the top photo on page 45)

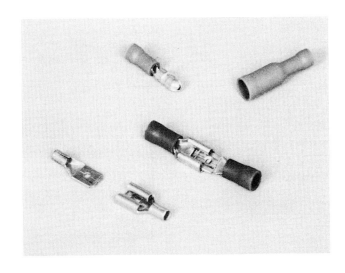

for most applications. They are also useful for connecting modular sections.

For low-amperage applications, such as lights, printed circuit board plugs are ideal. They are very small (right in the photo below left) and tricky to solder, but are perfect for large numbers of wires to a single location.

59 Wiring Accessories to Insulated Track Sections

is for a single wire, appropriate for the locomotive/tender type of jumper wire.

When more than one wire is routed to the same location, as with most accessories, multiple connectors are available (shown at left in the photo below). These come in two-, four- and six-wire configurations and are suitable

Insulated track sections may be made as described in Chapter One to operate automatic accessories. The diagram below shows how to wire a simple accessory, such as a crossing gate. Note that the wire from the transformer delivers fixed voltage to the accessory. The other wire is a ground, but it isn't grounded until a locomotive or car enters the insulated section of track. When this happens, the ground connection is carried from the insulated rail through the wheels of the car to the other outside rail of the track, which is connected to the ground of the transformer.

If you are using a simple transformer without fixed voltage circuits, simply connect the first wire of the accessory to the middle rail of the track (clip no. 1 on a lockon).

Some Lionel accessories, such as the no. 145 Gateman, have a light that stays on even when the accessory is not operating. This should be wired as shown in the diagram at

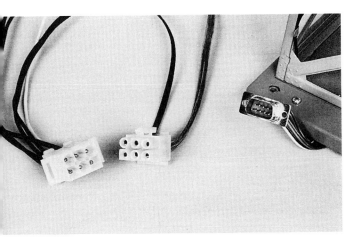

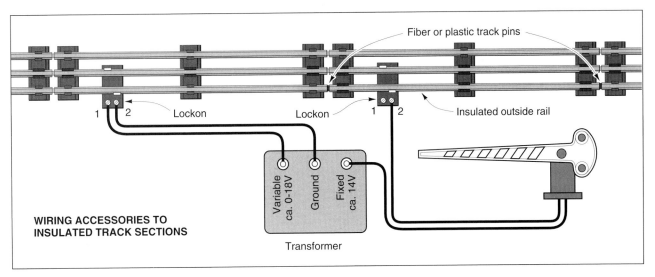

Fiber or plastic track pins

1 2 Lockon   Lockon 1 2

Insulated outside rail

Variable ca. 0-18V   Ground   Fixed ca. 14V

WIRING ACCESSORIES TO INSULATED TRACK SECTIONS

Transformer

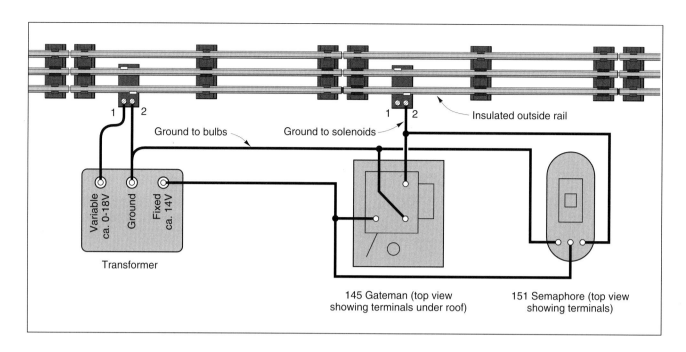

Ground to bulbs

Ground to solenoids

Insulated outside rail

Transformer

Variable ca. 0-18V | Ground | Fixed ca. 14V

145 Gateman (top view
showing terminals under roof)

151 Semaphore (top view
showing terminals)

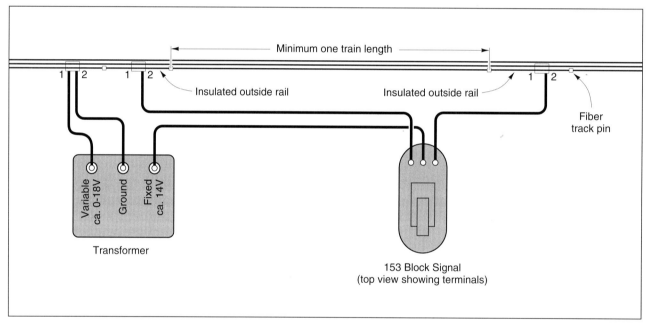

Minimum one train length

Insulated outside rail

Insulated outside rail

Fiber
track pin

Transformer

Variable ca. 0-18V | Ground | Fixed ca. 14V

153 Block Signal
(top view showing terminals)

the top of this page. The same procedure is used for a no. 151 Semaphore, also shown in the diagram.

Two insulated track sections can be used to light the red and green bulbs of a no. 153 Block Signal. The sections should be located at least one full train length apart, as shown in the diagram above. This method is more realistic than using a 153C contactor. With the contactor, one of the bulbs is lighted at all times, while with the insulated-rail method, the bulbs are lighted only when a train is in the vicinity, as in actual railroad practice.

If you use Lionel lockons for track connections, consult "Lionel Lockon Wiring Numbers" at the end of Chapter One for the proper way to wire these circuits.

60 Bidirectional Automatic Stop Station Circuit

Beginning in the middle 1930s, Lionel produced a variety of accessories and stations with train-stop circuits. Most common are the postwar nos. 115 and 132 stations, although many others are available from the prewar era, including the no. 078 signal and stations such as nos. 137, 134, and 136.

These thermostatically controlled devices are wired to a section of track in front of the station with an insulated middle rail. When a locomotive enters this section, no power reaches its middle rail pickups, and it stops. However, a trickle of current is routed through the heating coil of a bimetallic strip, which gradually bends and closes the circuit, so that after 10 to 20 seconds the locomotive starts automatically. On most devices, the period of time the train remains stationary is adjustable.

For the most realistic operation, the train should stop with the cars, not the locomotive, in front of the station. This would simulate, for example, coaches positioned at the platform to receive passengers. You can achieve this effect by wiring the stop device to a section of track a couple feet beyond the station, so that the locomotive proceeds far enough to put the cars in the right place before stopping.

However, if trains operate in both directions, this option will not work. If the insulated track is 2 feet to the left of the station, a train proceeding from the right will stop in the correct place, but a train coming from the left will stop far short of the station.

This problem is easily solved with a DPDT relay, as shown in the diagram below. Instead of one insulated section, the stop device is wired to *two*, one 2 feet to the left of the station and one 2 feet to the right. *Note that these sections must be less than one full train length apart.* Outboard of one of these insulated sections is a length of track with an insulated *outside* rail (see previous entry, "Wiring Accessories To Insulated Track Sections") wired as shown to trip the relay.

A train entering from the right causes the relay to provide current to the *nearest* section of track with an insulated middle rail. This keeps the locomotive running until it reaches the insulated middle rail on the *far* side, and the train stops with the cars in front of the station.

The same thing happens with a train coming from the left. The relay sends current to the left insulated middle rail, and the train continues until it reaches the right-hand section.

Any alternating current DPDT relay of appropriate voltage can be used. A 24-volt relay can be operated through a fixed-voltage post on a large transformer, such as the 20-volt post on a KW or posts B or C on a ZW, set to the highest voltage. A 12-volt AC relay will work with transformers of lower capacity, but these relays are harder to find. Direct current 12-volt relays are plentiful, and they will work with a Lionel transformer if fitted with a 50-volt full-wave bridge rectifier, as shown in the diagram.

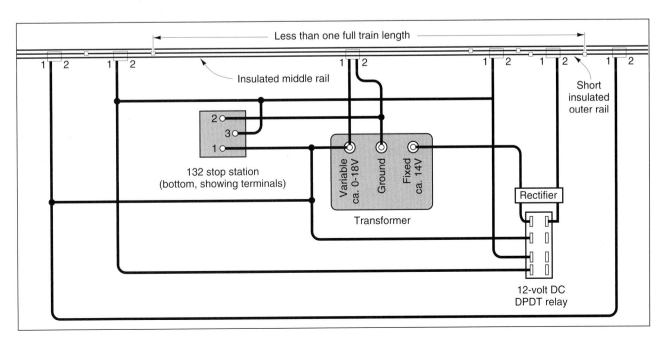

61 Wire Gauges

The word "gauge" has two principal meanings for the model railroader. First is the reference to the width between the rails. Most North American railroads are built to a gauge of 4'-8½" between the rails. Toy trains in O gauge run on track measuring 1¼" between the outside running rails, while Standard gauge trains run on track measuring 2⅛" between the outer rails.

The second significant meaning of the word "gauge" is to describe the thickness of wire. This thickness is measured by simple numbers, such as 18 gauge or 22 gauge. The higher the number, the thinner the wire will be; for example, 16 gauge wire is substantially thicker than 20 gauge.

The choice of what gauge to use in various applications depends upon the *current load* the wire will be required to carry and the *distance* over which that current must travel (in other words, the length of the wire).

Most toy train instructions specify 18 gauge wire for transformer-to-track hookups. This is adequate for small layouts, but for big pikes with lots of track, 18 gauge will not do the job. This is due to a phenomenon called "voltage drop." When current travels through wire, an amount directly proportional to the distance traveled and the diameter of the wire is lost. Since the distance cannot be reduced without making the layout smaller, the only available remedy is using larger-diameter wire.

For larger applications, such as a full-basement layout, wire of at least 14 gauge should prove more than satisfactory. One should not rely on the track alone to carry the current, as there is also considerable voltage drop through the pins of sectional track. Additional feeder wires should be routed directly to the more distant points on a layout.

Motorized accessories need nothing larger than 18 gauge wire in most cases, as they draw less current than locomotives, the real current hogs! For lighted accessories (signals, lampposts, etc.), 20 or even 22 gauge wire is usually sufficient, unless a large number are supplied with current on the same circuit.

62 Insulation Sleeves

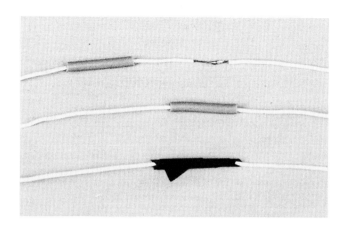

I am not a great fan of electrician's tape. Although it does a proper job of insulating soldered wire joints, the appearance seems to me to be less than professional. A neat and easy alternative is to strip short lengths of insulation from heavy gauge wire (12 or 14) and slip it over one of the wires to be soldered, as shown at top in the photo. After the joint cools, the piece of thicker insulation is slid down over the exposed wire until it covers it completely (photo at center). This looks much better than a joint wrapped with electrician's tape (bottom). In addition, if the joint ever needs to be removed, sliding the insulation off is easier than unwrapping the sticky tape.

63 Functional Telegraph Pole Wiring

Telegraph poles without wires are unconvincing, and while some modelers achieve satisfactory results with thread, I've always found that actual wire can be made to look quite realistic. More important, the wires can also be made functional.

Piano wire is the ideal choice. It comes in many different diameters and is stiff enough

to retain its shape. It can be bent to simulate the slight sag of wires between two poles, as shown in the photo, and it won't kink like thread. Best of all, it can be used to power your streetlights (see "Telegraph Pole Streetlights" in Chapter Three).

Thickness of the wire is a matter of personal choice. For the application shown in the photo, I chose relatively heavy wire because the layout is portable and is subject to vibration and mishaps during transport, setup, and teardown. Finer wire would look more realistic but would be less durable.

If you decide to give real wire a try, begin by drilling holes in the crossarms of the telegraph poles to receive the wire. Most commercial poles have very small insulators molded onto the crossarms. These insulators are not large enough to permit holes to be drilled in them, so place the holes in the crossarms just below the insulators. This slight discrepancy is barely noticeable. The holes should be small enough so the wires will stay in place by friction fit.

Bend a slight curve into each length of wire to simulate the sag between poles. Where two separate wires meet at the same pole, drill a slightly larger hole to accommodate both of them. If they fit tightly, they will maintain electric contact.

Piano wire is easily soldered, and electrical connections can be made wherever required. Several are visible in the photo. Not all of the wires on these poles are electrically live. Only two are needed for the streetlight circuit—one power wire and one ground. Take care to keep them from touching each other.

64 Barrier Strip Connectors

On simple layouts with a single connection to the track and few accessories, it is easy to wire everything directly to the transformer posts. However, as soon as we enlarge the pike to include sidings, blocks, and multiple train operation, or add more lighted or operating accessories, the number of wires expands

almost exponentially. For example, the massive amount of wiring shown in the photo above is for a relatively small layout: one main line, a passing siding, two reverse loops, seven uncoupling ramps, five switches, and a modest number of accessories.

On layouts like this, you need only *one* heavy wire from each transformer post. These are connected to insulated barrier strips (shown in both photos above), available at any electronics supply store. Then all layout connections are made from these barrier strips.

The construction of a barrier strip is simple. Each segment is made up of two electrically interconnected screws for attaching wires. Suppose, for example, you have six insulated blocks of track on the layout, each of which may be turned on and off by a toggle switch on the control panel. One wire, the transformer lead from the throttle rheostat, is connected to one screw on the barrier strip. A second wire connects to the other screw, as shown in the diagram, and leads to *all* of the toggle switches on the panel. These in turn are connected to the track blocks. This is much more efficient than having six separate wires from the six different toggles connected directly to the transformer.

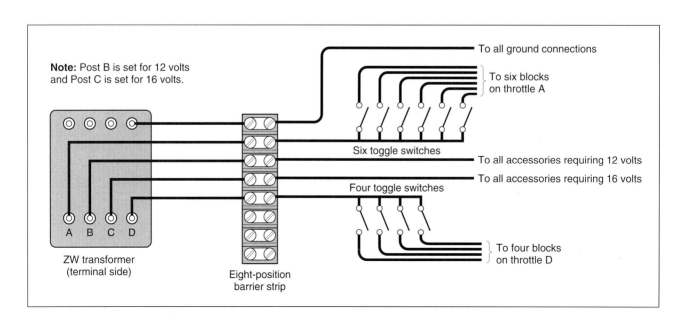

Note: Post B is set for 12 volts and Post C is set for 16 volts.

ZW transformer (terminal side)

Eight-position barrier strip

To all ground connections
To six blocks on throttle A
Six toggle switches
To all accessories requiring 12 volts
To all accessories requiring 16 volts
Four toggle switches
To four blocks on throttle D

Similarly, wires that come from the track or from accessories should never be connected directly to the toggles or other control switches on the main panel, but rather should be connected through barrier strips.

Since each of the various posts on a transformer may have more than one purpose in various combinations (variable and fixed voltage, two different levels of fixed voltage, etc.), the number of wires that would have to be attached to the transformer could be considerable. By using barrier strips, this number is drastically reduced, and everything is neater and easier to trace in case repairs are needed.

Another great advantage in using barrier strips is the ease of removing and replacing a defective transformer. Only one wire need be removed from each post, and it's easy to keep track of where to reattach them. Likewise a faulty accessory can be replaced by simply unscrewing the wires at the barrier strip. No unsoldering is required, and the toggle switch connections are unaffected.

The complexity of wiring needed for large train layouts can be greatly reduced by advance planning and careful attention to organization. A single wire can often be used in place of two or more, and barrier strips are the single greatest contributor to this systematic organization of the many components that go into even a relatively small Lionel pike.

65 Pipe Clamp Wire Supports

Hardware stores sell copper pipe supports. These are shaped like a half circle and have two holes for fastening to any wooden surface. They are ideal for grouping and routing wires under a layout, as shown in the photo (below left), and can be bent and shaped to suit almost any situation. Be sure, however, that the insulation on wires passing through them is adequate, since these pipe clamps conduct electricity and can cause short circuits. If in doubt, line them with electrician's tape.

66 Insulated Lug Wire Supports

Electrical supply stores sell solderless connectors (lugs) that can be attached to wires with a crimping tool. The larger ones have another use. They can serve as wire supports and guides, as shown in the photo above. Choose a lug which is large enough in diameter for the wire to pass through easily. Instead of stripping the wire and crimping it in the lug, just pass it through. Then, using the hole in the lug, screw it to the table wherever you want the wire to be held in place. It's neat and easy to remove if necessary.

67 Modifying Fixed-Voltage Circuits with Resistors

Most larger Lionel transformers have fixed-voltage posts for use with accessories, but the amount of current available varies from model to model. For example, the popular 1033 model can supply 5, 11, or 16 volts; the KW has three such circuits providing 6, 14, and 20 volts.

It would appear that these options could be used for almost any application, but this is not always the case. On the KW model, the most usable range, 14 volts, cannot be used with the transformer's common ground. Therefore, it won't work with any accessories that operate from an outside insulated rail. The 20-volt circuit uses the common ground, but 20 volts is too much for such units as crossing gates and semaphores. That much current would quickly burn out their light bulbs, as well as shorten the life of the solenoids. Operation would be much too fast and noisy.

It is relatively simple, however, to reduce the amount of voltage coming from any fixed-voltage post. Splice in heavy-duty resistors until the desired amount of power is obtained. For example, the 20-watt, 8-ohm resistor shown in the diagram below reduces 20 volts from a KW transformer to just the right level to supply the 022 switches on my layout. (Note that small resistors—¼ or ½ watt—intended for electronic uses will not work in these applications.)

You can determine the amount of voltage and amperage in these circuits with a test meter. If you don't have one, just experiment until you find a resistor or combination of resistors that gives you the desired results. Electronics supply houses carry a variety of 10- and 20-watt models; those with resistances from 1 to 8 ohms are most useful. For values in between, resistors can be wired in series.

68 Battery Operated Whistle and Horn Control

It's easy to make a horn or whistle switch for use with transformers such as models Z or R that don't have built-in whistle controllers. Lionel whistles and horns are turned on by a DC relay. When the whistle controller button is pushed, it superimposes a small amount of DC current, about 1½ volts, on the AC line to the track. This closes the relay that turns on the whistle motor or that turns on the battery-operated horn in a diesel.

The circuit shown in the diagram uses a 1½-volt D-cell battery to supply the DC current to close the relay. It is wired as shown through

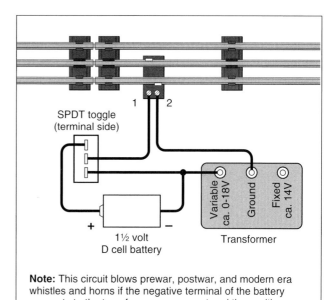

Note: This circuit blows prewar, postwar, and modern era whistles and horns if the negative terminal of the battery connects to the transformer power post and the positive terminal connects to the track through the SPDT toggle.

an SPDT toggle switch. This switch should not have a center-off position.

With the switch in one position, the AC current from the transformer goes directly to the track without passing through the battery. But throwing the switch in the opposite direction routes the AC through the battery, and the DC also passes to the track and trips the whistle or horn relay.

The toggle switch must be thrown quickly; if you throw it slowly, the layout may experience a momentary interruption of the current that will cause the E-unit reversing mechanism to operate.

This mechanism will also operate the electronic whistles, horns, and bells in modern era Lionel engines. However, polarity is critical. These mechanisms are dependent upon the polarity of the battery to operate. To control modern era whistles and horns, be sure the wire that connects to the track comes from the *positive* end of the battery, as the diagram on page 52 (right) shows.

If your locomotive has a bell in addition to the horn, it will be activated if the battery polarity is reversed, so that the *negative* end is connected to the track. This can be accomplished by wiring a battery into the circuit as shown in the diagram above right. The battery starts the bell ringing.

As soon as the bell begins ringing, the toggle switch should be thrown back to the direct-to-track position. To turn the bell off,

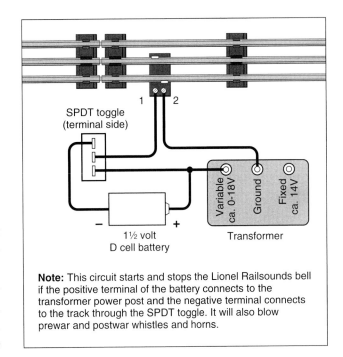

Note: This circuit starts and stops the Lionel Railsounds bell if the positive terminal of the battery connects to the transformer power post and the negative terminal connects to the track through the SPDT toggle. It will also blow prewar and postwar whistles and horns.

throw the SPDT again, then turn it off; the bell will stop ringing.

69 Using DC Relays with Lionel AC Transformers

If you are unable to find alternating current (AC) relays of the correct voltage rating for use with Lionel trains, the common 12-volt DC relay can be adapted. Purchase a 50-volt full-wave bridge rectifier, and wire it between the transformer and the relay. The diagram at

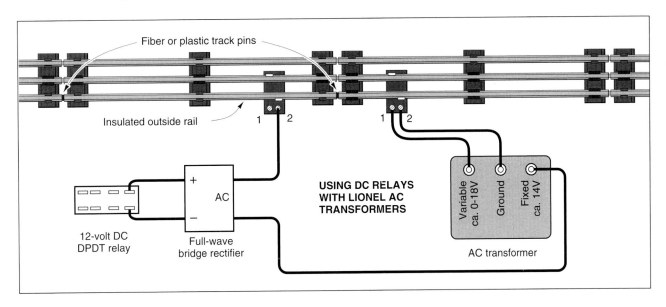

the bottom of page 53 shows just such a connection wired to a piece of track with an insulated outside rail. This circuit can be used to activate accessories, as explained earlier in this chapter ("Wiring Accessories To Insulated Track Sections") or for special applications such as trolley speed control (Chapter Two, "Automatic Circuit For Two Trolleys").

Chapter Five

SCENERY SCHEMES AND PAINT PRINCIPLES

*M*y mother always taught me that "appearances are deceiving," and she was right. Of course, the lesson she wanted me to learn was that I shouldn't judge people by what's on the surface, but this admonition also applies to toy train layouts. Lots of little tricks can create impressions of reality that both fool and delight the eye.

70 Paper Patterns for Scenery Construction

Take a tip from dressmakers. If you have to make any items of scenery that must fit in an irregularly shaped area of the layout, make a paper pattern first. Brown paper of the type used for wrapping packages comes in wide rolls, large enough for most scenic areas and stiff enough to lie firmly in place while you are working. The following tip describes one use for such patterns; others will undoubtedly occur to you.

71 Modular Grass Plots, à la Lionel

While the typical train layout has its scenery painted, textured, and sprinkled right on the table, this is a somewhat messy method and is not easy to modify. Lionel had the right idea with its scenic plots of the 1920s and '30s. These units came complete with grass, trees, shrubs, and such additions as houses, lampposts, sidewalks, and hedges where appropriate, mounted on a painted plywood or composition board base. These scenes could be moved to any location on a layout and endlessly rearranged to suit the operator.

Decorating a layout in this manner is easy and lends a delightful period appearance, especially when used with prewar tinplate trains. Once the track has been laid and wired, make a paper pattern of the area where the plot will go, as shown in the top photo on page 56. On a piece of ¼" plywood, transfer the pattern using carbon paper or cutting out the pattern and tracing around its edge. Cut out the base with a handheld jigsaw or saber saw.

Where the plot is to butt against a building or a raised roadway, cut it at a 90-degree

angle. If it is to form a terrace or sloping lawn edge, cut it at a 45-degree angle. Remember that a jigsaw will produce the smoothest cut edge on the *underside;* therefore, the pattern should be *reversed* and traced upside down.

When the plywood is cut out and turned over, it will fit properly and have the smoothest edges facing upward. Test-fit the piece and make any adjustments before painting by planing and sanding the edges wherever necessary.

Next sand the entire surface; if the whole area is to be lawn, paint it with two coats of green latex, approximately the same color as the grass. When this has dried, give it a thick third coat and immediately sprinkle lots of grass all over it, then let it dry thoroughly. Finally, shake off the excess and save it for the next plot. The grass will adhere wherever it touched wet paint.

If you want sidewalks or driveways on a plot, first paint it with two coats of a concrete color instead of green. When it is completely dry, use masking tape to cover any area where you don't want grass. (On the plot shown here, masking tape was used to create a curb and a sidewalk, separated by a narrow grass strip.) Then add a coat of green paint, let it dry, paint on another coat, and sprinkle the grass as explained above.

Install the plot on the layout. It may simply be set in place or fastened permanently by driving short screws through the tabletop from beneath and into the underside of the plot. Be sure to choose screws that are just long enough to hold tightly, but not so long as to penetrate the top surface. Alternatively, you can screw the plot down from above and

countersink the screw heads. To hide the heads, cover them with a thick drop of green paint and sprinkle grass over them while the paint is still wet.

The kind of wood chosen for these plots depends on the texture desired. Smooth, cabinet-grade plywood faced with such woods as birch are expensive but make beautiful golf-green lawns. Particle board or chipboard makes a rougher surface, and the grass will adhere in a less regular fashion, more like a vacant lot. Experiment with different materials and choose those that suit your taste (see tip no. 72). Cheap grades of plywood should be avoided, as they tend to warp out of shape and will not lie flat on the layout. Small plots work best. They are easily cut to fit and less likely to warp.

Grass materials are available in a variety of colors from hobby shops or architectural supply houses and range from very fine to coarse. The grass on my Standard gauge layout (see photo on page 58) came from an authentic bag

of Lionel grass, appropriate to the period atmosphere of this period railroad. You can even make your own by sifting sawdust and dying it, but this is a time-consuming job, and it is difficult to obtain convincing colors. With so many good materials on the market at reasonable cost, making your own grass is an unnecessary chore.

One nice feature of these plots is the way they create the illusion of a ditch along the roadbed, where the beveled edge slopes downward. But the real advantage of this system will become apparent the first time you change the layout. Just remove the plot, rearrange your track or buildings or whatever, and make a new plot to fit. You won't have to scrape the scenery off the surface of the layout or clean up the mess.

Best of all, most of the work can be done while sitting in a comfortable chair at the workbench, rather than stretching to some nearly inaccessible point on the layout. Modular scenery is fast and easy, and produces very satisfying results.

72 Uses for Spruce Underlay

Building-supply houses sell 4-foot-square sheets of ¼" spruce plywood intended as floor underlay. This is an excellent product for making grass plots (see previous entry) and other scenic details. It is relatively smooth, sands easily, and can be made even smoother by applying sanding sealer to the surface. It cuts easily with a hand-held power saw, can be cut into almost any shape, and is simple to work with hand tools. And the size of these sheets is quite manageable.

One of our portable layouts has a hidden reverse loop underneath the main table. A simulated stone retaining wall, shown in the photo on the next page, hides the track that descends to the loop. We made the wall from spruce underlay cut to shape and fitted with a stripwood cap. We painted the cap gray and then sprayed it with Speckle Stone Imitation Granite Spray Paint (see tip no. 73) to simulate concrete.

We applied printed sheets with a simulated stone pattern to the face of the wall. These are manufactured by Faller and are available at hobby shops. Alternatively, the entire wall could be painted to represent concrete. The landfill behind the wall is made from foam, also discussed later in this chapter.

Of course, any ¼" plywood can be substituted for the spruce underlay, but the very low price and convenient, easy-to-manage 4-foot-square size of the sheets make it ideal for scenery. In addition, one side is smoother than the other. This gives the builder a choice of textures for scenic plots.

73 Easy Imitation Ballast

There are many ways to simulate ballast on a layout, most of them messy. They range from commercially available scale-size particles to plain old Kitty Litter, but each requires some sort of glue to keep it in place. Ballast is also difficult to keep dust-free and is hard to remove from the track when you decide to change the layout.

A product is available in hardware or paint stores that simulates the appearance, and to a lesser degree even the texture, of ballasted right-of-way. Called Speckle Stone Imitation Granite spray paint, it is marketed by Home Hardware in Canada in 16-ounce aerosol

cans. There are similar products available in the United States, sold in aerosol form and in larger quantities for compressed air sprayers. The paint comes in colors ranging from light gray through medium brown to almost black and contains flecks of light-colored material that give the surface a slightly rough, variegated appearance.

The easiest and most economical way to use this product is to paint the area with two latex base coats of the approximate shade of the speckled paint, which is sprayed on as the

final coat. If you don't use a raised roadbed, spray the entire table; then the track can be mounted anywhere. This is much easier than trying to measure in advance exactly where the track will be. If you lay your track on cork roadbed, as shown in the lower right photo on page 59, paint it with the base color after installation, spray it with the speckled paint, then install the track.

The rest of the scenery can be added after the track is in place and wired. Put masking tape about ½" from the ends of the ties and add your grass and other details, then peel off the tape for a sharp edge along the roadbed.

This ballast paint doesn't have quite the depth or texture of Kitty-Litter ballast, of course, but at least you won't have to worry about Fluffy mistaking the layout for her sanitary facilities.

74 Scenic Circuit Breaker

Lionel's no. 91 Circuit Breaker doubles nicely as a scenic accessory next to a Power Station. If you are using a modern transformer with a built-in circuit breaker, bypass the internal wiring in this accessory and wire it so the bulb

stays lighted at all times. For variety, install a red blinking bulb.

75 Foam Scenery

For many, many years, the most common way of building mountains and tunnels on model railroads involved making wooden or cardboard forms covered with wire screening. This in turn was coated with cloth or paper soaked in plaster of Paris, then carved to simulate terrain. This extremely messy method gave way to hard-shell techniques in the 1960s, a big improvement certainly, but still slow and wet.

A much easier way to build a mountain is to carve scenery from high-density foam insulation panels. Available in 4 x 8 sheets from building supply houses in various thicknesses up to 4", these panels can be stacked together with carpenter's glue for taller walls or mountains. Their light weight makes handling easy. The high-density type is easy to carve with a sharp knife, and cracks and seams can be filled with drywall crack filler. Ledges, paths, and streams can be carved into the surface wherever wanted. The end result can be as plain or as elaborate as the builder's artistic skills permit.

(While proofreading this manuscript, my wife reminded me that I should recommend acquiring a large supply of adhesive bandage strips before carving foam scenery. For some

reason, I rarely manage to finish a mountain or a valley without slicing off small portions of my epidermis in the process.)

76 Instant Water

Most hardware and building supply stores sell 2 x 4 panels of translucent plastic for covering ceiling fluorescent light panels. They come in various textures, including a pebbled version that looks remarkably like the wind-blown surface of a river or a lake.

Prepare a subsurface support board by painting it to represent the color of water—blue for a deep lake, closer to gray for most rivers and streams. Spot-glue the translucent panel over the painted board and put it in place. Presto: instant lake!

The lake area on my Standard gauge layout doubles as a removable access hatch. I used some high-density, lightweight foam for the support board; plywood will work, too. For a more convincing appearance, decorate the shoreline with weeds and half-submerged logs, and put a rowboat in the middle. One manufacturer of O scale figures (Arttista, 1616 S. Franklin St., Philadelphia, PA 19148) even makes swimmers, cut in half for placement on the surface of the water.

77 Cork Trestle Supports

Lionel's nos. 110 and 111 trestle sets provide an easy, inexpensive method of adding elevated track to a layout. The trestles are easy to install, as they come with track supports that make it easy to mount each trestle bent at the point where two track sections join. However, when used in this manner they give a layout an unfinished appearance. Although the rails are sturdy enough to support a train as it passes from bent to bent, the ties look as if they are just hanging in space beneath the rails.

To give the appearance of stringers between the bents, cut strips of cork and attach them to the bottoms of the ties with contact cement. I use half strips of N gauge cork roadbed for this purpose. The cork is flexible and will conform to curves in the track, and using contact cement (according to directions on the tube or can) makes it unnecessary to clamp the strips in place until they dry.

GarGraves flexible track gives a more convincing appearance than regular sectional track, but adding these cork strips to any kind of track takes away the bare look of an unsupported line. Adding extra ties between the metal ones helps, too. These can be made from stained wood or can be purchased commercially. Moondog Express (1245 Riverview Drive, Fallbrook, CA 92028-1851) makes black rubber ties for both O gauge and O-27, as well as for American Flyer S gauge.

78 Rubber Cement for Residue-Free Adhesion

Rubber cement is a handy substance for placing details on a layout that might be moved frequently. It works just like contact cement. You place a thin coat on both surfaces to be joined (the feet of a figure and the spot where it will stand, for example), let them dry a few seconds, then touch them together.

The advantage of rubber cement over regular contact cement is ease of removal when a figure or other detail is moved. While contact cement must be scraped off, rubber cement can be rolled off without leaving any trace on most surfaces. It's neat, clean, and easy!

79 Covered Crossing Gate Ramps

Shortly before the Second World War, both Lionel and American Flyer began producing nearly scale-sized crossing gates, mounted on ramps that simulate grade crossings. Flyer continued production of its handsome no. 591 gate after the war, but Lionel's nos. 46 and 47 models were not made after 1942. However, many can still be found, and they look much better on an O or S gauge layout than the more common oversized gates such as Lionel's no. 252.

Unfortunately, the roadway area of these gates was painted a light beige, which looks wrong with simulated asphalt or concrete roads. Since most toy train operators are reluctant to paint their vintage accessories (and rightly so, since it decreases their value), a less permanent way to change the color of these crossing gate ramps is needed.

Stationery stores sell thin tag report covers, such as those made by Duo-Tang, in a variety of colors. The black shade is a close match for asphalt, and there's a gray color that looks something like concrete. These can be cut, folded, and placed over the gate ramps as shown in the photo on the next page. Nor must they be glued in place; just

surface but not enough to go all the way through. This produces a straight, even bend on the reverse side.

80 Convincing Model Trees

Most modelers are well aware of the line of scenic materials manufactured by Woodland Scenics (P.O. Box 98, Linn Creek, MO 65052). Their line includes good-looking trees made of plastic or white metal with ground foam foliage. The larger sizes look good on Lionel O gauge layouts.

If you want greater variety in your miniature forests, look to the architectural supply houses. These firms make trees and bushes in a wide variety of shapes, sizes, and colors. They include conifers, hardwoods, colors for spring and fall foliage, and even fruit trees in bloom. The trees shown in the photo below came from Accurate Dimensionals (4185 S. Fox St., Englewood, CO 80110.)

cut them slightly longer than necessary, and fold the ends under the pieces of road, or back under the base of the gate itself.

To get a really crisp fold, lightly score the underside of the tag material with a modeler's knife, just enough to penetrate the

81 Cutting Moondog Roads

Moondog Express (1245 Riverview Drive, Fallbrook, CA 92028-1851) manufactures an easy-to-use line of imitation asphalt streets. Made of a flexible rubberized material in straight and curved sections of various lengths, as well as intersections, the roads are printed with a center line and several different warnings, such as "SLOW" and "RXR" (Railroad Crossing).

The shapes provided are adaptable to many different street configurations without modification, but they can also be cut to fit in special situations. Getting a really clean edge, however, requires a special technique.

Use a new blade in your modeler's knife; a no. 11 works best. Use a straightedge as a guide, or if you have to make a curved piece, cut a wooden jig in the correct shape. Holding the knife absolutely vertical, draw it *very lightly* along the guide, just barely penetrating the surface of the road. The next cut may be slightly deeper, but the secret to a really sharp edge is a series of many very light passes with

the knife. Trying to cut too deeply pulls and stretches the rubber material and leaves a ragged edge.

Moondog Express periodically publishes an interesting newsletter, which contains instructions for using their products. Following their advice will make your streets and parking lots extra-realistic.

82 Keeping Freight Car Doors Closed

If you'll allow me a slight digression from scenery, I'd like to pass on the solution to a small problem that really annoys me. I hate to see a string of boxcars passing by on the layout with their doors partly open. (With the hobo problem I have on my pike, keeping these doors secure is essential!) The motion of the train sets up vibrations that cause these doors to slide back and forth.

My wife's mom, Mrs. Gertrude Bull, gets the credit for this one. She uses a length of broomstick to immobilize the sliding glass doors that lead to her deck, and seeing her drop it into place one evening suggested to me that the same trick could be used for freight car doors. Just cut a thin piece of strip-wood or styrene to the proper length, and drop it into the lower door guide. This will keep unwanted riders out of your rolling stock and present a much neater appearance as the trains pass by.

83 Hiding Accessory Terminal Screws

This is another tip that seems almost too obvious, but it's amazing how many layouts I've seen where the appearance of the scenery is marred by those ubiquitous terminal nuts that Lionel provided for the attachment of wires. They're easy to hide—plant a bush over them! Lichen or ground foam from a commercial supplier works fine.

84 Painted Tunnel Portals

In 1957, Lionel began marketing plastic tunnel portals with molded stone and concrete block details. The early models had "HILLSIDE" embossed across the top and "1957" on one side of the base. The modern era equivalent carries "LIONEL" across the top instead.

The "HILLSIDE" version is collectible and not nearly as plentiful. Also, it is a darker,

more realistic color than the pale gray of the newer portals. While I don't recommend altering the appearance of the "HILLSIDE" models, you can make your "LIONEL" portals look much better by spraying them with the Speckle Stone Imitation Granite spray paint described earlier in this chapter under the heading "Easy Imitation Ballast." Similar portals, such as the ones shown in the photo, are available from Antique Trains, 1 Lantern Lane, Turnersville, NJ 08012.

85 Inexpensive Bake Oven

To achieve a durable paint job when restoring old tinplate trains, each coat should be baked for 20 minutes to half an hour at about 200 to 250 degrees F. I caution you, however, not to use the household oven for this task, unless you live alone and have little or no olfactory sense. The smell of baked enamel is persistent and obnoxious, and the one time I used our kitchen appliance for this purpose, it was four days before the air returned to normal. My wife's reaction was unprintable!

Fortunately, no elaborate equipment is needed to create an efficient oven. Mount two

simple sockets fitted with 60-watt bulbs inside a wooden crate, wire them in parallel to an extension cord, and provide a loose cover that can be placed over the top. The crate in the photo measures about 14" x 14" x 12", adequate for most O gauge projects.

Get an inexpensive thermometer that reads up to 500 degrees F. to keep track of the heat being produced. If the cover closes off the box completely, the oven will get too hot, so it should be placed so as to leave an air vent, as shown in the photo below. Experiment with the size of the vent space until a temperature of approximately 250 degrees F. is obtained. This will cure paint in a half hour or less, but

be careful not to let the oven get hotter, as it may cause the finish to scorch or craze.

While painted metal parts may be baked without risk, plastic parts need special attention, as heat can melt or warp them. Use a lower level of heat and a longer baking period for plastics. If in doubt, experiment with scrap plastic until you are sure what level of heat is safe.

86 The Least Expensive Bake Oven

I discovered this one when I was about 11 years old. I had two old bicycles that badly needed new paint jobs. In the early 1950s, the wonderful modern acrylic enamels had not yet appeared, and I knew little about how to achieve a smooth, hard coat with the type of paint available then.

I started this project on a warm, clear day with almost no wind. On the first bike, I applied a beautiful shade of royal blue and left it out in the sun to dry. Within just a few hours, the finish was completely dry and glistening. The next day I painted bike number two a brilliant red and expected the same results. After 24 hours, the finish was still tacky, and rather than being smooth and hard, it was speckled with little dust particles that ruined the shine and made it rough to the touch.

The reason wasn't hard to figure out; the second bike was painted on a cool, cloudy day when the humidity was high and the wind was blowing. While the first bike was baked quickly by the sun, the second one was left to air-dry in a relatively damp atmosphere. The long drying time, combined with gusts of wind that pelted the bike with dust and dirt, spoiled my efforts.

Toy trains will also bake very nicely in the hot sun, with no cost for electricity. Choose a calm, still day and put up wind baffles just in case of stray gusts. It isn't even necessary that all surfaces face the sun. The metal will warm up enough so that the paint on the underside will also bake hard, although a little more slowly. No temperature control is necessary. The sun's heat will not exceed safe levels for enamel or acrylic paint or lacquer.

87 Automobile Touch-up Paint for Toy Trains

There are some fine enamels on the market that closely replicate original Lionel, Ives, and American Flyer colors. My favorite brand is produced by Charles Wood of Classic Model Trains, P.O. Box 179, Hartford, OH 44424.

While I always use Charlie's paint for such colors as Peacock, Mojave, Stephen Girard Green, and other specialized colors, there is another source of excellent paint for the many generic shades of reds, browns, and silvers used on many toy trains: automobile touch-up paint lacquer. The range of shades is extremely wide, and it dries quickly and is very durable. And the small spray cans are economical and just the right size for the average toy train project.

88 Dry Transfer Lettering

Most prewar Lionel, Ives, and American Flyer trains were lettered with rubber stamps, and this technique was carried over to some postwar items as well. There are suppliers who make authentic reproduction rubber stamps that duplicate this original process, but acquiring separate stamps for every model can be quite expensive.

A much more economical alternative is dry transfer lettering. The most extensive line for these products is available from Janice Bennett of Bennett Dry Transfers, P.O. Box 178, Closter, NJ 07624. Janice is licensed by Lionel Trains, Inc., so there is no problem of copyright infringement when using her products.

The lettering comes printed on a translucent sheet that allows you to see exactly where it is being positioned on the trains. Rubbing on the back of the sheet releases the letters and causes them to adhere to the metal or plastic sides of cars or locomotives. A special burnishing tool is made especially for this purpose and can be purchased from artist supply stores. Any small, smooth tool, such as a ball point pen, will also work.

To set the letters firmly, a second translucent sheet, provided as a safety backing to the lettering sheet, is placed over the transferred letters and then rubbed with the same tool, or with something larger such as the smooth end of a table knife. Again, artist supply stores sell a special rounded spatula that does this job safely and easily.

Detailed instructions come with Janice's catalog, which also lists decals and stripes for Lionel postwar trains.

89 Easy Tinplate Paint Removal

You may not believe this one! The first time I heard it, I was frankly very skeptical, but it works beautifully. I only wish I had known about it years ago, as it would have saved me the cost of much paint stripper, countless pairs of rubber gloves, and a lot of guilt over damage to the environment. The paint on old tinplate trains and accessories can be removed completely with *plain laundry detergent and boiling water!*

Winston Lill, formerly with Greenberg Publishing, passed the idea on to me, but he credits Bruce Greenberg with the concept. Get a large pot (I use a roasting pan) that you won't need for any other purpose, as it will be stained from the paint. Fill it with enough water to cover the item to be stripped, boil the water, and add half a cup of your favorite detergent. Drop in the tinplate train and watch the paint lift off! Use a pair of tongs to retrieve the now naked tinplate, and scrub it with a brush to remove any clinging bits of paint. Then rinse it off in clear water, dry it to prevent rust, and it's ready for repainting.

A word of caution: this process works on

tinplate only, since plastic trains will warp alarmingly if boiled.

90 Repairing Castings with Plastic Metal

It is not unusual to find trains and accessories from the early 1920s through the 1930s that have deteriorated in some respect. Most common are crumbled drive wheels on locomotives of all manufacturers, and even the pilot and trailing wheels on American Flyer engines. Fortunately, reproduction wheels are readily available.

A more serious problem is encountered with cast locomotive or accessory *bodies*. The majority of Dorfan locomotives, for example, are found warped and pitted, or with chunks of the bodies broken off; some have even crumbled to dust. The magnificent Ives Standard gauge steam locomotives and tenders of the late 1920s are similarly affected. Cast accessories from all manufacturers are also frequently found in a deteriorated condition.

The problem is impurities in the molten zinc that was poured into the molds to make the castings. The reaction of these impurities with the zinc has caused the metal to break down with age. Manufacturers soon discovered the problem, and by the later 1930s, the material was more carefully mixed to eliminate foreign substances. The best of these old toys show no damage whatever, but many have small pits or cracks that detract from their appearance.

These imperfections can be filled with a substance available in tubes from auto supply stores: Plastic Metal. This material, when squeezed into cracks or depressions, hardens within a few hours to almost the same strength as the casting. After curing, it can be filed to match the contours of the locomotive or accessory. If carefully worked, these repairs will be virtually invisible after painting.

91 Painting Prewar Zinc Castings

Zinc castings are also notoriously difficult to paint. Some will take a finish coat beautifully, but since they are porous and often contain impurities, paint sprayed on some of them tends to bubble up, especially when baked. This effect can be reduced or eliminated by application of at least three coats of a good quality red oxide primer applied before the finish coats.

These castings should not be baked at a high temperature; sun baking (see entry no. 86, above) is usually hot enough and will not cause the surface to bubble if the primer has been properly applied. To be absolutely sure, air dry the painted surfaces for several days in an area where the humidity is low. The finish won't be as hard as if it were baked, but it will remain smooth.

92 Inexpensive Painting Supports

It's easy to build supports from scrap wood that will allow you to spray-paint all surfaces of a toy train from all angles. Custom build them to suit the shapes of the parts you are painting. Use thin screws or brads to hold the parts to the support. For small items, such as window frames, bend thin wire into hangers.

These supports are easily hand held and can be turned so that all sides of the parts can be sprayed evenly. Be sure the supports are well balanced so that they will stand upright in the oven during the baking process.

93 Protecting Hands from Paint

The cheapest, most convenient gloves for use while spray-painting are available from the drug store. Plastic surgical gloves come in several different sizes and are extremely thin so that finger sensitivity is maintained. They can be used over and over.

These gloves are tight fitting and do not "breathe"; therefore, your hands tend to sweat while wearing them. To lessen this discomfort, dust on a little talcum powder before you put them on.

94 Realistic Colors for Telephone Poles

If the plastic telephone poles on your layout were installed just as they came out of the package, the color is probably all wrong. Most of these toy accessories are molded in shiny dark brown plastic and look nothing like real telephone or power-line poles

In my home province of Nova Scotia, the light and power company uses mostly spruce for its poles, and while they may be brown when first installed, they quickly weather to a mellow driftwood gray. To simulate this on a layout, I sprayed my poles with Mojave paint, the same color used on a large number of Lionel trains in the 1920s and early '30s. The result is a pleasant shade, somewhere between tan and gray, that looks exactly like the real telephone poles I see every day.

Chapter Six

TOOL TRICKS AND CONSTRUCTION CONCEPTS

Having the right tools, and using them correctly, can turn tedious chores into pleasurable accomplishments. What follows are some suggestions regarding tools you may want to own, techniques you may want to try, and ideas you may want to consider.

95 Soldering Iron Oxidation

Whether for connecting wires or for joining metal parts such as carbody panels, secure solder joints are vital to the success of many construction and wiring efforts. Unfortunately, a cold solder joint can be the source of frustrating and hard-to-diagnose problems.

The success of any solder joint depends upon the temperature of the surfaces to be joined being high enough to melt the solder. It is not enough to heat the solder itself. For two wires or parts to be joined together, both must be heated sufficiently so that the solder melts and flows into the joint *without* the soldering iron actually touching the solder. Only in this way can one be sure that the solder will adhere properly. If either surface is not hot enough to melt the solder thoroughly, the joint will fail.

After prolonged use, soldering irons and guns seem to lose their effectiveness. This is

most often caused by oxidation between the tip and the socket or sockets in which the tip is mounted. On a gun, loosen the screws or collars that hold the tip and remove it. File the working end of the tip to remove accumulated solder, flux, dirt, and oxidation. File the shanks of the tip where they fit into the gun, or polish them with emery paper, and reinsert. Tighten the screws or collars securely, and the gun will operate at maximum temperature again.

If you are using an iron, loosen the screw that holds the tip in place, then remove it. File the tip as above, both the working end and the shank, and replace it in the iron, fastening the screw tightly.

96 Choosing a Soldering Iron

For electrical work, especially projects that involve miniature electronic parts, a low-power soldering iron (25–35 watts) is recommended. Such tools are less likely to fry delicate components than the heavier-duty 75–100 watt irons. Although much more convenient, soldering guns are seldom recommended for electronic applications, since they can generate enough heat to damage transistors, printed circuits, and the like.

However, the convenience of guns is a powerful argument in their favor. A soldering iron takes much longer than a gun to reach operating temperature and retains a lot of heat after being unplugged. The gun cools much more quickly and is, therefore, safer when resting on the workbench.

During any layout-building project, soldering jobs are normally interspersed with other chores. It might take 20 minutes to route the wires from track to control panel, and only half a minute to solder the connections. It is a waste of electricity (and potentially hazardous if you are as likely as I am to knock the darn thing off its stand onto the floor) to leave a soldering iron plugged in for a long time in anticipation of brief usage.

But plugging the soldering iron in and unplugging it every time is annoying, especially given the time it takes to heat up, so I use a gun for all connections on the layout itself. That way the gun is ready to use just a few seconds after turning it on, and yet it cools off quickly enough to prevent burns from accidental contact with the skin. (Be especially careful when connecting wires to miniature toggle switches, as they will not stand much heat, and their plastic cases can become distorted from high temperatures.)

There are many solid-state devices now on the market for model railroad use. Since their components are susceptible to heat damage, I save all work on these units for a single workbench session, and I stick to the low-powered iron. I solder short wire leads to their contacts, and when installing these devices on the layout, I use mechanical connectors (crimp-on lugs, for example), thus avoiding the inconvenience and discomfort of soldering with a slow-to-heat iron while I am underneath the train table.

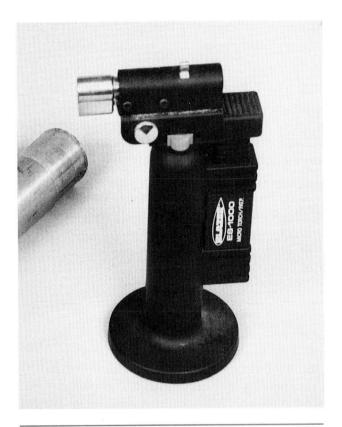

97 Joining Metals: A Superior Torch

This tip comes from Garry Condon of Kentville, Nova Scotia. Garry is not a toy train collector or operator; his profession is dentistry. However, he never fails to ask about my involvement in the hobby, and when he discovered a versatile new tool with applications in his profession, he inquired whether I might find it useful. This tool turned out to be one of the most convenient and efficient I've ever used.

The Blazer ES-1000 Self-Igniting Micro Torch (The Blazer Corporation, 114 E. 32nd St., New York, NY 10016) is a lightweight, handheld, refillable torch with an infinitely variable pinpoint flame, capable of generating temperatures up to 2500 degrees F. (1300 degrees C.). The torch stands upright on a stable round base, giving a horizontal flame, or it can be balanced on its back to provide a vertical flame.

Garry uses the torch for denture work. It's also useful for jewelry-making, and opticians use it to adjust eyeglass frames. In the toy train hobby, it solders, brazes, and removes paint. I've found it valuable for soldering small parts, as the pinpoint flame makes it possible to attach a small detail quickly without overheating an entire structure and possibly loosening other solder joints.

The Blazer allows a modeler to use both hands, but it can also be handheld and directed into hard-to-reach spots, such as inside locomotive or tinplate car bodies. It lights instantly by means of a pushbutton and has a safety automatic on-off control. The flame can be made fine or full, depending upon needs. It's a great addition to the hobby workbench.

98 Save Your Clothes, Skin, and Eyes

This may seem too obvious to mention, but I and most modelers of my acquaintance have learned this lesson the hard way. If you have to make overhead soldering connections from underneath a layout, be sure you are wearing old clothes and that no skin is exposed. A single drop of solder can wreck your good jeans or dress slacks or burn a nasty hole in your epidermis. Perhaps even more important, be sure to wear safety glasses.

The best solution is to avoid soldering under the layout completely, as discussed in Chapter Four under the heading "Solderless Wiring Connections."

99 Pliers That Work in Reverse

Toy train repairers often find that they need a tool that exerts pressure *outward*, as when spreading the sides of an E-unit. There is a clever item that accomplishes this task, called a retaining ring tool, available at any hardware store. Squeezing the handles together moves the jaws of the tool in the direction opposite to that in which regular pliers function.

A similar tool, available at auto supply outlets, is intended to remove piston rings. This

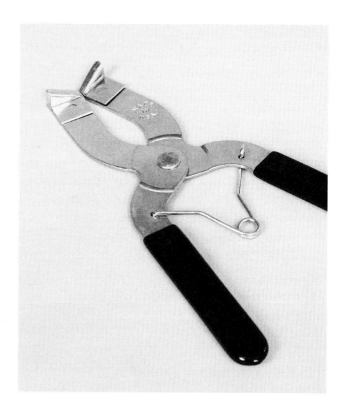

piston ring remover is somewhat sturdier than the retaining ring tool, but the width of the jaws makes it difficult to insert into tight spaces, such as between the sides of a motor frame. However, the jaws can be filed down to fit. Anyone who has ever tried to spread the sides of a Lionel motor with a screwdriver will appreciate the wonderful advantages these tools afford.

100 Safety Glasses

The eyes are among the most easily damaged organs in the body, and model railroaders are especially vulnerable to ocular accidents. Many of our tasks involve close attention to small details, and the eyes are often right in the line of fire when a screwdriver slips, a metal sliver flies out of the jaws of a snipper, or a little hot flux splashes from a solder joint.

Putting a layer of plastic between your eyes and your work is cheap insurance. Without this protection, a second's slip of the hand can mean a lifetime suffering the effects of eye damage.

101 Lightweight Table Construction

There are several ways to build toy train layout tables, the most common of which are the *tabletop* and the *cookie cutter* style. These concepts have been thoroughly explored in the model railroad press and in several specialty books available in hobby stores. There's a third method that offers great simplicity, speed, rigidity, and portability with few drawbacks.

Hollow-core doors are available in a variety of widths at building supply stores. The length is a standard 6'-8", and they measure about 1¼" thick. This size is ideal for a modular layout: the light weight makes them easy to handle, the surface is smooth, and the construction eliminates any possibility of warping. Best of all, no supporting framework is needed.

You can build conventional legs from lumber, but the easiest solution is a set of folding legs, as shown in the photo above. Because the door is hollow, you will need lengths of 1 x 2 or 1 x 3 strapping to mount them. Fasten the strapping at points around the perimeter of the door where it is solid, and screw the legs to the strapping. Any number of tables can be placed side by side to make a layout, and wiring can be transferred from table to table by quick-disconnect plugs (see Chapter Four).

The table shown in the photo is for our portable layout, which loads easily into a station wagon for trips to train meets and local schools. If you are building a permanent layout, fasten the tables together and omit the quick-disconnect plugs.

There are several disadvantages, of course. These doors amplify the noise of the trains during operation, as the hollow core acts like a sounding board. And the hollow core makes it a little harder to feed wires through from the top to the underside. (Put a lamp under the table, and the light shining through will help you find the wiring holes more easily.) Also, on portable layouts it is difficult to disguise the joints between tables. But the advantages are too great to ignore, especially the speed with which a roomful of tables can be built.

102 Rollaway Transformers

Most of us are not blessed with unlimited room for a train layout, especially when the layout room doubles as a workshop and repair center. It is convenient to get those bulky Lionel transformers out of the way under the layout when not in use.

Build a simple rollaway table as shown in

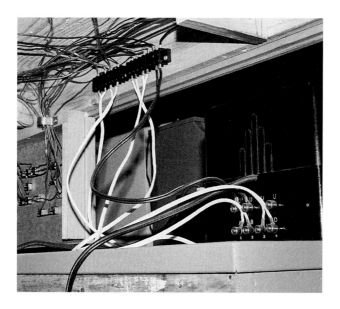

the photo on page 73. The frame is made from 1 x 3 spruce, the top is a plywood panel edged with outside corner molding, and the sides are pegboard. One flexible wire is routed from each terminal of each transformer to a terminal strip under the layout as shown in the photo above. Make the wires long enough to allow the table to be moved. Lamp cord is excellent for this purpose, as it is flexible and heavy enough to prevent voltage drop.

Mount a power bar under the table, and plug all the transformers into it. Splice a toggle switch into the line cord of the power strip and locate it on the front of the rollaway table. Use a toggle or power strip with a pilot light to remind you to turn the transformers off when you're finished operating.

103 Disappearing Transformer Platform

An alternative to the rollaway transformer table is the swing-away model shown in the photos. Two ZW models are fastened to a ¾" plywood board. Two 1 x 3 spruce arms support the board and are pivoted beneath the table on ¼" stove bolts. A hinged length of spruce is cut to the proper length to support the board when in the upright position.

When in use, the board swings up and out to a horizontal position, thus putting the

transformers in a handy position in front of the train table. After the operating session, the hinged support is folded upward, and the platform swings to a vertical position, completely under the table and out of the way.

104 An Efficient Work Area

A train repair center need not be large; mine occupies a tiny corner of the layout room only a few feet square. The central element is a

workbench made from an inexpensive unfinished desk. On the top is a short length of Lionel O gauge track with an uncoupling ramp, wired to a no. 1033 transformer. Two test leads ending in alligator clips are also connected to the transformer. A test meter (volts/ohms) with flexible test leads is permanently fastened at right.

Above the bench is a plastic tool rack mounted on the wall. On the adjacent wall are several multidrawer storage cabinets for small parts. Next to them (out of sight in the photo) is a set of steel shelves holding larger parts, spray paint, and other essential items. The key to efficiency in such a small place is organization. The better the organization, the more space you will have for the layout itself.

105 Fast and Easy Display Shelves

Fancy oak or walnut display shelves make a beautiful backdrop for a train collection, but having them built can cost big bucks. A quick and easy alternative can be made from ready-made strip pine paneling, 3½" wide, available in building supply centers.

I used simple L-angles to mount the shelves shown in the photo. For a more formal location, you might prefer wooden supports. The shelves themselves are left their natural pine color, finished in liquid urethane for durability. The panels have grooves in them cut lengthwise to hold the train wheels in line. This eliminates the need for mounting track on the shelves or putting a raised guard on the edge to keep them from falling off.

106 A Third Hand

The original blueprint for human beings obviously never anticipated the hobby of model railroading; otherwise it would have included three hands, possibly even four, as original equipment. It seems that practically every

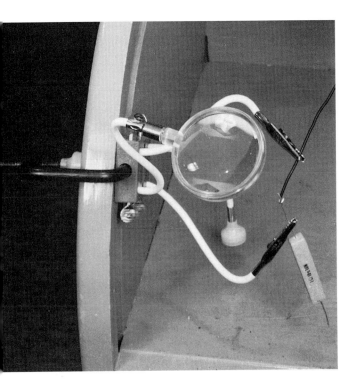

chore requires more than the usual quota of two. Consider, for example, the simple task of soldering. One hand holds the pieces of the work together, another holds the hot iron, and we're left with nothing but our teeth to maneuver the solder against the joint.

Extra hands are available from a radio or electrical supply store, in the form of alligator clips. Mount a pair of them on a wooden base, side by side and facing each other at a 45-degree angle. They do a great job of holding two wires or pieces of metal together, leaving you free to handle the solder and the iron with ease and safety. For more complex jobs, use more clips.

If you wish, there's a commercial version, called the Professional Helping Hand, available from hobby shops. It's a clever and inexpensive set of four flexible alligator clips mounted on a base that can be clamped to the workbench. It also features an adjustable magnifying glass for those of us whose eyesight is not quite up to putting Z scale apples on the trees in our orchards.

In Conclusion . . .

This completes our review of helpful tips, some simple and some rather ingenious, that can make toy train operation more rewarding. Better yet, they save time that is better spent running trains.

Every modeler probably has similar ideas that the rest of us would like to hear about. If you would like to share your knowledge, please send me your tips for inclusion in the next edition of this book. The address is Kalmbach Publishing Co., P.O. Box 1612, Waukesha, WI 53187-1612. Happy railroading!

Pete Riddle
Kentville, Nova Scotia

Index

ABOUT THE AUTHOR

Peter Riddle can legitimately claim a life-long involvement with toy trains, for his family's first Lionel set arrived on Christmas in 1939, just four days before he was born. This little freight set, a no. 229 locomotive with three cars and a loop of track, later gave way to a succession of HO layouts, a brief excursion into O scale, and finally an extensive toy train collection that Pete shares with his wife, Gay. At present, the Riddles have seven separate layouts, spanning more than 90 years of toy train history.

In addition, Pete and Gay have a portable layout they take to schools to introduce a new generation of youngsters to the joy of toy trains. With its tunnels and hidden loops of track, this "Magic Railroad" delights young people with disappearing trains and a variety of operating accessories that the youngsters can control themselves, thanks to pushbuttons located around the perimeter of the table.

Peter teaches in the School of Music at Acadia University at the rank of full professor. He also served as administrative head of the school for nine years and is a published composer of music for concert and jazz bands, chamber ensembles, and soloists. His latest book in the field of music is a text on the topic of instrumental conducting.

Greenberg Publishing Co. currently offers Pete's four earlier books about toy trains. There are two volumes of *Wiring Your Lionel Layout* that instruct readers in all aspects of basic electrical principles and practices. *Trains From Grandfather's Attic* is a colorful volume that describes the author's building techniques for prewar trains, and *Greenberg's Guide To Lionel Trains, 1901–1942, Volume III, Accessories* is a thorough exploration of the many signals, bridges, buildings, and other scenic accessories that Lionel produced during its first four decades of production.

The Riddles have two grown children, Kendrick and Anne.